I0071630

another 100 Mental Models

volume 2

100 MENTAL MODELS
TO HELP YOUR CAREER

COEVOLUTION

OODA LOOP

SELF-DISTANCING

R/K SELECTION THEORY

CHESSBOARD THINKING

PSYCHOLOGICAL CAPITAL

POWER OF WEAK TIES

ENCLOTHED COGNITION

KILL CRITERIA

T-SHAPED PEOPLE

PRATFALL EFFECT

STRUCTURAL HOLE

DIFFUSION OF INNOVATIONS

FAT-TAILED DISTRIBUTION

REPRESENTATIVENESS HEURISTIC

PYGMALION EFFECT

FALSE CAUSALITY

RESILIENCE BANKING

THE SERENITY PRAYER MODEL

COGNITIVE LOAD THEORY

PARKINSON'S LAW OF TRIVIALITY

MONTE CARLO SIMULATION

BY DAN WAITE

and many many more

ANOTHER 100 MENTAL MODELS TO HELP YOUR CAREER – Volume 2

BY DAN WAITE

Published by Loco Tempus Limited 2025

Copyright Dan Waite 2025

Cover design by Dan Waite

British Library Cataloguing in Publication Data

A catalogue record for this book is available from the British Library

ISBN: 978-1-917784-15-3

ISBN   978-1-9177841-5-3

9 781917 784153 >

This is dedicated to my wife Irena, my family & friends and work colleagues, present and past.

With thanks to Ade Adeluwoye, Nicolas Bate for your life changing Personal Excellence course, Allen Kovac for your trust and guidance as a boss and mentor and Napolean Hill for the advice in spotting opportunity in hard work.

In memory of my father David Waite.

Hi, I'm Dan Waite, CEO of Better Noise Music.

I've long been fascinated by cognitive and mental models—although I didn't known that is what they were collectively called until much later.

My home library is packed with books on the subject, and some models are so impactful they've inspired the author to write an entire book on just one idea.

Volume 2 of this book is the result of an ongoing exchange of ideas with my good friend Ade Adeluwoye. We regularly share book recommendations that help us grow as individuals and leaders.

The first book contained some of the mental models I first learned during my early days at Virgin Records, from mentors like my Chairman, Allen Kovac, and that I've discovered more recently—through platforms like X (formerly Twitter), thought leaders like Elon Musk, and deep dives of my own.

This book pushes beyond those first 100, and is now takes us to 200 mental models in total. (Although if you get to the 100th model and beyond 100 you will discover Positive Surprise Asymmetry).

I hope you find these models as insightful and energizing to explore as I did while researching and compiling them. And keep an eye out—Volume 3 is on its way soon. Dan Waite

Other books in this 100 series – scan here

100 Cognitive And Mental Models To Help Your Career: Mental Shortcuts for Smarter Choices, Sharper Thinking, and Success

-

ANOTHER 100 MENTAL MODELS TO HELP YOUR CAREER - VOLUME 2: Another 100 Powerful Mental Models for Clarity, Confidence, and Climbing the Career Ladder

-

100 HEURISTICS AND HEURISTIC MODELS: The Hidden Rules of Smart Thinking Used by Experts, Entrepreneurs, and Machines

-

100 Game Theories And Decision Models For Rational Decision Making In Competitive Situations: 100 Winning Strategies for Rational Thinking in High-Stakes Scenarios

-

100 Business Strategies Proven Tactics For Growth, Innovation And Market Domination: Actionable Strategies to Scale, Disrupt and Lead in Any Industry

-

100 Leadership Models And Strategies For Effective Decision-making For Organizational Success: Empowering Your Leadership, 100 Proven Strategies and Models to Enhance Decision-Making & Drive Success

-

100 Business Growth Hacks And Strategies To Grow Profit And Increase Your Competitive Advantage: Proven Techniques to Scale Faster, Boost Revenue, and Dominate Your Market with Actionable Growth

-

100 ECONOMIC THEORIES DEMYSTIFIED : A Guide To The World's Most Influential Economic Ideas From Keynesian Economics To Debt-deflation Theory

-

100 Passive Income Stream Side Hustles, Mastering Side Hustles And Smart Investments: How to Make Money While You Sleep and Secure Your Financial Future

-

ANOTHER 100 MENTAL MODELS TO HELP YOUR CAREER

BY DAN WAITE

Cognitive and Psychological Models:

1. Cognitive Load Theory – The mind can only process limited information at once. p 15

2. Availability Cascade – A self-reinforcing cycle where repeated information seems more credible. p18

3. False Causality–Mistaking correlation for causation p21

4. Empathy Gap – Difficulty in predicting others' emotions or future emotional states. p24

5. Illusion of Control – Overestimating our ability to control events. p27

6. Restraint Bias – Overestimating one's ability to resist temptation. p30

7. Peak-End Rule – We judge experiences based on their peak and end moments. p33

8. Representativeness Heuristic – Basing judgments on stereotypes rather than probabilities. p36

9. Salience Bias – The most noticeable information disproportionately affects decisions. p39

10. Self-Handicapping – Creating excuses in advance to protect self-esteem. p42

Economic and Financial Models:

11. Law of One Price – Identical goods should sell for the same price in different markets. p 45

12. Giffen Goods – Higher prices increase demand for certain products. p 48

13. Prisoner's Dilemma (Iterated) – Cooperation evolves through repeated interactions. p 51

14. Zero-Based Thinking – Re-evaluate decisions from scratch, as if no prior investment existed. p 54

15. Path of Least Resistance – Resources follow the simplest route. p57

16. Creative Accounting – Using legal loopholes to manipulate financial data. p60

17. Velocity of Innovation – The rate at which new ideas spread and are adopted. p 63

18. Fat-Tailed Distribution – Rare events occur more often than normal distributions predict. p 66

19. Efficient Market Hypothesis – All known information is reflected in asset prices. p 69

20. Boomerang Effect – Attempting to change behaviour can sometimes reinforce the opposite. p 72

Systems and Physics Models:

21. Critical Point – A system's tipping point where a small change causes a major shift. p 75

22. Diffusion of Innovations – The spread of new ideas follows predictable patterns. p 78

23. Tipping Point – The threshold where gradual buildup triggers significant change. p 81

24. Bottleneck Effect – A limiting factor restricts overall system performance. p 84

25. Convergence – Different systems evolve to produce similar outcomes. p 87

26. Emergence – Simple interactions lead to complex systems. p 90

27. Kinetic Energy of Ideas – Ideas gain momentum and become unstoppable once widely accepted. p 93

28. Structural Hole – Gaps in networks represent untapped opportunities. p 96

29. Information Asymmetry – One party knows more than the other in a transaction. p 99

30. Punctuated Equilibrium – Systems remain stable until rapid shifts occur. p 102

Social and Psychological Models:

31. Tribalism – People align strongly with groups and resist outsiders. p 105

32. Pratfall Effect – Imperfections make people more relatable and likable. p 108

Mathematical and Logical Models:

44. Logarithmic Growth – Progress slows over time, requiring greater effort for smaller returns. p 144

45. Exponential Decay – Diminishing returns set in rapidly. p 147

.46. Inverse Relationship – As one variable rises, another falls. p 150

47. Decision Trees – Visualizing choices and consequences improves clarity. p 153

48. Monte Carlo Simulation – Random sampling predicts complex systems. p 156

49. Bell Curve (Normal Distribution) – Most data falls around an average, with extremes being rare. p 159

50. Symmetry Breaking – Small asymmetries lead to significant differences. p 162

Leadership and Management Models:

51. Span of Control – Efficiency depends on how many direct reports a manager oversees. p 165

52. Pygmalion Effect – Higher expectations lead to better performance. p 168

53. Theory X & Theory Y – Management styles are shaped by assumptions about employees' motivations p171

54. Parkinson's Law of Triviality – Teams waste time on unimportant details. p 174

55. Lean Thinking – Eliminate waste to improve efficiency. p 177

56. T-shaped People – Deep expertise in one area combined with broad knowledge. p 180

57. Open-Loop vs. Closed-Loop – Systems improve faster when feedback is continuous. p183

58. Bullwhip Effect – Small changes upstream lead to large disruptions downstream. p 187

59. Six Sigma – Reducing variability improves quality P190

60. Minimum Viable Product (MVP) – Launch a basic version and iterate. p 193

Biological and Evolutionary Models:

61. Survival of the Fittest – Those best adapted to environments thrive. p 196

62. Mutualism – Different species benefit from cooperation. p 199

63. Coevolution – Species evolve in response to each other. p 203

64. Genetic Drift – Random events shape evolution. P207

65. Mimicry – Organisms imitate others to gain advantage. p 210

66. Ecosystem Thinking – Systems interact in complex, interdependent ways. p 214

67. R/K Selection Theory – Different reproductive strategies lead to survival. p 218

68. Homeostasis – Systems self-regulate to maintain balance. p 222

69. Critical Mass in Biology – Populations must reach a certain size to survive. p 226

70. Life History Theory – Organisms allocate energy to growth, reproduction, or survival. p 230

Philosophical and Ethical Models:

71. Moral Relativism – Morality is shaped by culture and context. p 234

72. Utilitarianism – Maximize happiness for the greatest number. P238

73. Deontology Follow rules regardless of outcomes. P242

74. Virtue Ethics Character shapes moral behaviour. p 245

75. Social Contract – Society exists based on mutual agreement. p 248

76. Stoicism – Focus on what you can control, accept what you cannot. p 252

77. Existentialism – Individuals create their own meaning. p 256

78. Golden Mean – Virtue lies between extremes. p 259

79. Occasionalism – God directly causes all events. p 263

80. Libertarianism – Maximize individual freedom. p 266

Strategic Thinking and Problem-Solving Models:

81. Strategy vs. Tactics – Strategy is the overarching plan; tactics are the actions to achieve it. p 270

82. OODA Loop – Observe, Orient, Decide, Act – a rapid decision-making cycle. p 273

83. Sunken Ship Fallacy – Abandon ventures that no longer serve a purpose. p 277

84. First Mover Advantage – Being the first in a market often creates dominance. p 281

85. Fast Follower Strategy – Let pioneers test markets, then replicate and improve. p 284

86. Strategic Depth – Having multiple layers of backup plans. p 288

87. Kill Criteria – Clear, pre-set conditions to abandon a project. p 291

88. War of Attrition – Victory goes to the one who can endure the longest. p 294

89. Chessboard Thinking – Plan multiple moves ahead to anticipate consequences. p 297

90. Decoy Effect – Introducing a less desirable option to drive choice towards a preferred one. p 301

Psychological Resilience Models:

Cognitive and Psychological Models:

1. Cognitive Load Theory

Mental Model and Cognitive Load Theory: A Breakdown

Theory

Mental models are internal representations of how things work in the real world. They help individuals understand systems, predict outcomes, and solve problems by simulating scenarios in their minds. In the context of **Cognitive Load Theory (CLT)**, mental models play a crucial role in managing cognitive resources. CLT, developed by John Sweller, asserts that working memory has a limited capacity. Learning becomes more effective when instruction aligns with how learners mentally represent and process information.

Mental models reduce **intrinsic cognitive load** by helping learners chunk complex information into meaningful patterns. They also minimize **extraneous load** when instruction complements or builds upon these internal structures. In turn, this promotes **germane load**—the effort devoted to developing and refining mental models.

Example

Imagine teaching someone how to operate a manual transmission car. Instead of overwhelming them with technical jargon about torque, gears, and clutch plates, you explain it using a bicycle analogy: "Changing gears in a car is like shifting gears on a bike when going uphill or downhill." This familiar framework (mental model of bike gears) simplifies new, complex content by mapping it onto prior knowledge.

Why It Works
Mental models reduce the cognitive burden by linking new information to existing schemas in long-term memory. This facilitates faster processing, better retention, and more efficient problem-solving. When learners can simulate how a system works based on their mental model, they require less mental effort to understand or apply new information.

How It Works
Instructional strategies that foster mental model development often use analogies, simulations, visual aids, and storytelling. These tools help students form structured representations of how systems operate. For example, flowcharts in programming or circuit diagrams in electronics support learners in building accurate mental models. Once these models are established, they guide reasoning and decision-making with less strain on working memory.

Application
Mental models are widely used in education, user interface design, aviation, and healthcare training. In classrooms, teachers scaffold new knowledge using prior experiences. In software design, intuitive interfaces mimic real-world tools (e.g., digital folders resembling paper folders), leveraging users' mental models to ease navigation.

Key Insights

- Effective instruction builds on what learners already know.

- Misaligned mental models can lead to misconceptions and higher cognitive load.

- Repeated exposure, feedback, and varied examples help refine mental models.

- Teaching should make abstract concepts concrete through relatable analogies.

Conclusion

Integrating mental models into instruction, guided by Cognitive Load Theory, leads to deeper understanding, efficient learning, and better knowledge transfer by aligning teaching with the brain's natural information processing limits.

2. Availability Cascade

Mental Model: Availability Cascade – A Breakdown

Theory

The **Availability Cascade** is a concept introduced by Timur Kuran and Cass Sunstein. It describes a self-reinforcing cycle where repeated public exposure to an idea makes it seem more credible, not because of its truth, but due to its *availability* in collective memory. This is rooted in the **availability heuristic**—a cognitive bias where people judge the probability or importance of something based on how easily examples come to mind.

An availability cascade begins when a claim—regardless of its accuracy—gains attention through media, social discourse, or authority figures. As more people discuss and share it, social pressure to conform grows, reinforcing belief and fuelling further spread. Eventually, the belief can become widespread "common knowledge," often influencing public opinion or policy, even in the absence of solid evidence.

Example

Consider the fear around vaccines and autism. A now-discredited study once linked the MMR vaccine to autism. Although the research was flawed and retracted, the claim gained traction through media repetition and public discussion. As more people heard and repeated it, the fear felt more plausible. Despite scientific evidence debunking the link, the availability cascade fuelled a widespread antivaccine movement, showing how misinformation can gain lasting traction.

Why It Works

The availability cascade works because our brains are wired to conserve energy. Repetition of an idea makes it easier to retrieve and process, leading us to believe it must be important or true. Additionally, social proof—seeing others accept the idea—further validates it in our minds. In uncertain situations, we default to what feels familiar or commonly accepted, even if irrational.

How It Works

- A provocative or emotionally charged idea gains initial attention.

- Media and social amplification increase its presence.

- People begin repeating the idea, often without scrutiny.

- Repetition builds familiarity and perceived legitimacy.

- Social dynamics pressure dissenters to stay silent, further solidifying the belief.

Application

Understanding availability cascades is critical in media literacy, public policy, and crisis communication. It explains why urban myths, conspiracy theories, or moral panics spread rapidly. Policymakers, journalists, and educators can use this model to anticipate and counteract misinformation by intervening early with clear, repeated, evidence-based messaging.

Key Insights

- Popularity ≠ truth; repeated exposure can distort perception.

- Emotional triggers (fear, outrage) fuel the cascade effect.

- Countering cascades requires repetition of accurate information, not just facts.

- Awareness of the model helps individuals become more discerning thinkers.

Conclusion

The Availability Cascade shows how easily repetition can shape collective belief. Recognizing this mental model helps guard against bias, misinformation, and manipulated narratives in our increasingly media-saturated world.

3. False Causality

Mental Model: False Causality – A Breakdown

Theory

False causality, also known as **post hoc ergo propter hoc ("after this, therefore because of this"),** is a logical fallacy where a cause-and-effect relationship is incorrectly inferred between two events simply because they occur in sequence or appear correlated. This mental model highlights how easily the human mind assumes causation when only correlation or coincidence exists.

In decision-making and reasoning, false causality leads to flawed conclusions. People often link outcomes to preceding events without investigating alternative explanations or underlying mechanisms. This model is deeply connected to **cognitive biases** like pattern recognition and the desire for clear explanations, especially in complex or uncertain situations.

Example

Imagine a school introduces a new math curriculum, and standardized test scores rise the following year. School officials claim the curriculum caused the improvement. However, this may be a case of false causality. Other factors—such as increased tutoring, changes in student demographics, or teaching quality—may have contributed.

Without controlled analysis, the conclusion about
causation is premature.

Why It Works
False causality appeals to our natural desire to make sense
of the world. Our brains are wired to recognize patterns
and assign meaning. When two things happen together or
in sequence, it feels intuitively correct to link them.
Emotion also plays a role—causal stories are more
satisfying than admitting "we don't know." This makes false
causality easy to believe and hard to disprove.

How It Works

- An event (A) is followed by another (B).

- The human mind seeks explanation and assumes A
  caused B.

- Without further evidence, the causal claim spreads
  and becomes accepted.

- Confirmation bias then reinforces the belief, as
  people notice instances that support the cause-
  effect link and ignore those that contradict it.

Application
False causality is especially relevant in areas like
journalism, marketing, medicine, and public policy. In
advertising, a product is shown solving a problem (e.g.,
"after using this cream, my acne disappeared"), even
though improvement may have occurred naturally or due
to other factors. In healthcare, anecdotal testimonials

often mislead people into believing a treatment works without scientific backing.

Key Insights

- Correlation does not imply causation.

- Strong claims require controlled evidence and multiple variables to be ruled out.

- False causality can influence public opinion, spread misinformation, and lead to poor decision-making.

- Critical thinking and scepticism are essential tools against this fallacy.

Conclusion

Understanding the false causality mental model helps individuals think more critically, ask better questions, and avoid drawing faulty conclusions in a world overflowing with coincidental data and persuasive narratives.

4. Empathy Gap

Mental Model: Empathy Gap – A Breakdown

Theory

The **Empathy Gap**, a concept rooted in behavioural psychology and decision science, refers to our tendency to underestimate the influence of emotional and physiological states—either in ourselves or others—on thoughts, decisions, and behaviours. It's part of the broader field of **hot-cold empathy gaps**, where "hot" states are emotional, impulsive, or stressed, and "cold" states are rational and calm.

People in a "cold" state struggle to predict how they'll feel or behave in a "hot" state, and vice versa. This gap in empathy creates blind spots in judgment, leading to poor decision-making, ineffective communication, or unrealistic expectations of oneself and others.

Example

Consider someone making a plan to eat healthier and avoid junk food. In a calm, well-fed (cold) state, they believe it will be easy to resist temptation. But when they are hungry, tired, or stressed (hot state), their resolve weakens. The earlier plan fails, not because of lack of willpower, but because they failed to anticipate how their emotional state would alter their decision-making.

Why It Works

The empathy gap works because our brains compartmentalize emotional and rational thinking. When in one state, we lack access to the full intensity or perspective of the other. This leads to a kind of "state-dependent blindness." It's easier to judge others—or even our future selves—based on logic, overlooking how much emotional context shapes action.

How It Works

- A person in a "cold" state makes decisions, sets goals, or judges others.

- When transitioning into a "hot" state (anger, desire, pain), those previous assessments no longer seem relevant or realistic.

- The person either acts against their prior judgment or misinterprets others' behaviours due to emotional disconnect.

- After returning to a cold state, they often regret or fail to understand their own actions.

Application

Understanding the empathy gap is vital in healthcare, education, negotiation, addiction recovery, and conflict resolution. For instance, doctors advising patients on pain management must recognize that someone not currently in pain may underestimate how it affects decision-making. Likewise, policymakers designing interventions for drug use or financial planning should anticipate how stress or craving alters rationality.

Key Insights

- Self-control strategies should account for future emotional states.

- To bridge empathy gaps, simulate or recall intense emotional experiences.

- Avoid judging others without considering their emotional context.

- Planning and behaviour change are more effective when emotional variability is expected and addressed.

Conclusion

The Empathy Gap highlights the limits of our understanding—of ourselves and others—across emotional states. Recognizing and planning for this disconnection leads to better decisions, deeper empathy, and more realistic expectations in real-world interactions.

5. Illusion of Control

Mental Model: Illusion of Control – A Breakdown

Theory

The **Illusion of Control** is a cognitive bias where individuals overestimate their ability to influence outcomes that are largely or entirely determined by chance. Coined by psychologist Ellen Langer in 1975, this mental model highlights how people believe they have control over situations purely because they are involved or have taken some action—regardless of whether that action affects the result.

This illusion often arises in uncertain environments and is reinforced by randomness, patterns, or previous successes. It is particularly prevalent in gambling, financial markets, sports, and leadership contexts, where people mistake involvement or familiarity for influence.

Example

A classic example occurs in gambling. Imagine someone rolling dice at a casino. Many believe that throwing the dice harder will yield higher numbers or that they're "due for a win" after a losing streak. In reality, each roll is independent and random. Despite this, gamblers often feel they can influence the outcome through rituals, timing, or technique—demonstrating the illusion of control.

Why It Works

The illusion of control stems from our psychological need for certainty and agency. Humans are pattern-seeking by nature. When we experience a win or success after a certain action—even by chance—we tend to attribute it to our behaviour rather than randomness. This false feedback loop reinforces the belief that we can influence outcomes. It also helps protect our ego by giving us a sense of mastery in uncertain situations.

How It Works

- A person takes action in a scenario governed by chance.

- A favourable outcome follows, often by coincidence.

- The person attributes success to their action rather than randomness.

- Over time, this leads to overconfidence and riskier decisions.

- Failure is often rationalized as a fluke, not as evidence of lack of control.

Application

The illusion of control is seen in business decisions, investing, leadership, and even everyday life. Traders may attribute market gains to their skill rather than market conditions. Managers may believe their leadership alone drives team performance, ignoring external factors.

Understanding this model can prevent overconfidence and encourage data-driven decisions.

Key Insights

- Perceived control boosts confidence but can distort judgment.

- Recognizing randomness helps manage risk and expectation.

- Effective decision-making requires separating influence from illusion.

- Systems thinking and evidence-based feedback help counter this bias.

Conclusion

The Illusion of Control reminds us that confidence isn't always grounded in reality. By distinguishing between actual influence and perceived control, we can make smarter decisions, reduce errors, and better navigate uncertainty in personal and professional life.

6. Restraint Bias

Mental Model: Restraint Bias – A Breakdown

Theory

Restraint Bias is a cognitive bias where people overestimate their ability to resist temptation or control impulsive behaviour. This mental model is closely tied to emotional self-regulation and is often observed in addiction psychology, behavioural economics, and self-discipline research. The bias leads individuals to believe they are less vulnerable to temptation than they actually are, causing them to expose themselves to situations they would be better off avoiding.

This overconfidence can result in poor decision-making, as people misjudge their future behaviour—particularly when transitioning from a calm (cold) state to an emotionally aroused or impulsive (hot) state. Restraint Bias is a key contributor to self-control failures, because it prevents individuals from putting effective safeguards in place.

Example

A common example is found in digital addiction. A student may believe they can study while their phone is next to them, insisting, "I won't check it." However, once a notification pops up, the temptation proves too strong. Despite their earlier confidence, the student is repeatedly distracted. Their failure stems not from a lack of discipline, but from a false belief in their ability to resist a predictable impulse.

Why It Works

Restraint Bias works because people judge future scenarios based on their current state of mind. When calm and removed from temptation, they underestimate the emotional pull that future temptations will exert. This is compounded by a desire to see oneself as in control and rational. Admitting susceptibility can feel uncomfortable, so we unconsciously deny it.

How It Works

- In a non-triggering state, a person believes they can handle a future temptation.

- They engage in risky planning or remove protective barriers.

- When temptation arises, emotional impulses override rational intentions.

- They give in, often followed by regret or rationalization.

- The cycle repeats, reinforced by continued overconfidence.

Application

Restraint Bias has applications in addiction recovery, financial planning, dieting, and productivity. Tools like pre-commitment (e.g., blocking websites, limiting cash access, or scheduling obligations) help by removing the need for willpower in the moment. In therapy and behaviour change programs, acknowledging restraint bias leads to better long-term strategies for impulse control.

Key Insights

- Avoiding temptation is more effective than resisting it.

- Planning should assume you'll be weaker in the moment than you feel now.

- Pre-commitment and environmental design are powerful tools.

- Self-awareness of limits fosters more effective decision-making.

Conclusion

Restraint Bias reminds us that self-control is situational, not constant. Recognizing and planning around our vulnerabilities enables better habits, healthier choices, and fewer regrets.

7. Peak-End Rule

Mental Model: Peak-End Rule – A Breakdown

Theory

The **Peak-End Rule** is a psychological heuristic identified by Daniel Kahneman and Barbara Fredrickson. It suggests that people judge an experience largely based on how they felt at its **most intense moment** (the *peak*) and **how it ended**, rather than the total or average experience. This applies to both positive and negative events and has a powerful effect on how we remember and evaluate past experiences.

Rather than objectively assessing an event's full duration or cumulative effect, the brain simplifies the memory by focusing on the standout moments—especially the emotional high point and the final impression. This can distort how we later reflect on decisions, relationships, or experiences.

Example

Consider two patients undergoing a colonoscopy. One has a shorter but more painful procedure that ends abruptly, while the other endures a longer procedure, but the pain gradually lessens toward the end. Interestingly, patients tend to rate the second experience as less unpleasant in retrospect—even though it lasted longer—because the *end* was more comfortable and the *peak* pain less extreme.

The overall duration becomes less important in memory than the emotional peaks and conclusions.

Why It Works

The Peak-End Rule works because the human brain prioritizes **emotional salience** over accuracy in memory formation. We compress experiences into snapshots—especially those charged with strong emotions or endings—because it's more efficient for decision-making. Evolutionarily, this may have helped humans recall key events (like danger or pleasure) to inform future choices.

How It Works

- During an experience, multiple emotional states are registered.

- When recalling the event, the brain doesn't access all of these equally.

- It emphasizes the emotional *peak* (best or worst moment) and the *ending*.

- These two moments heavily influence how we rate the overall experience.

- This recalled evaluation shapes future decisions (e.g., whether to repeat the experience).

Application

This model is vital in fields like customer service, education, healthcare, entertainment, and UX design. A restaurant visit might be mediocre overall, but if the dessert is fantastic and the service warm at the end, customers will likely return. Similarly, a teacher who ends each lesson with an engaging summary or uplifting note can leave students with a lasting positive impression, regardless of earlier challenges.

Key Insights

- First impressions matter, but final impressions often matter more.

- A strong emotional moment can define an entire experience in memory.

- End well—even if the start or middle was flawed.

- Memory is not an average; it's a highlight reel.

Conclusion

The Peak-End Rule reminds us that how we *remember* an experience matters more than the full experience itself. Designing moments with emotional peaks and strong finishes can shape perception, satisfaction, and long-term behaviour.

8. Representativeness Heuristic

Mental Model: Representativeness Heuristic – A Breakdown

Theory

The **Representativeness Heuristic** is a cognitive shortcut where people assess the probability or truth of something based on how much it resembles an existing mental prototype, rather than relying on statistical reasoning or logic. Coined by psychologists Amos Tversky and Daniel Kahneman, this heuristic causes us to ignore base rates, probability, and real-world data in favour of pattern matching.

It's the mental model behind snap judgments like "he looks like a professor, so he must be one" or "this company's logo looks professional, so the service must be high quality." While this can sometimes lead to accurate judgments, it frequently results in **biases and logical errors**, especially when dealing with randomness or complex systems.

Example

Imagine you meet Tom, who is quiet, organized, loves books, and enjoys working alone. If asked whether Tom is more likely to be a librarian or a farmer, most people would say librarian—because Tom matches the stereotype. However, this ignores the base rates: in many countries, farmers vastly outnumber librarians. Statistically, Tom is more likely to be a farmer, but our brains default to the more "representative" image.

Why It Works

The representativeness heuristic works because it reduces mental effort. Our brains are wired to recognize patterns quickly, especially ones that fit our existing schemas or stereotypes. This fast, intuitive processing evolved for survival, helping us make quick judgments in uncertain or dangerous situations. But in modern, data-driven contexts, this can lead us astray.

How It Works

- We encounter a person, event, or scenario.

- We unconsciously compare it to a mental prototype or stereotype.

- If it matches closely, we judge it as more likely or valid.

- We ignore statistical evidence or logical reasoning if it conflicts with the match.

- The more vivid or detailed the description, the more convincing the match seems—even if it's irrelevant to actual probability.

Application

Understanding this mental model is critical in hiring, investing, jury decisions, and everyday judgment. In hiring, for instance, someone who "looks the part" may be favoured over a more qualified but less stereotypical candidate. In investing, a company with flashy branding might seem successful even if its fundamentals are weak.

Key Insights

- People often confuse similarity with probability.

- Stereotypes can distort rational thinking, even when statistically incorrect.

- Detailed or vivid stories can overpower data in influencing belief.

- Being aware of base rates and statistical reasoning is essential in countering this bias.

Conclusion

The Representativeness Heuristic shows how easily our minds can be tricked by appearances. Recognizing this bias helps us question surface judgments and make decisions rooted in evidence, not intuition alone.

9. Salience Bias

Mental Model: Salience Bias – A Breakdown

Theory

Salience Bias is a cognitive bias where individuals focus their attention disproportionately on information or elements that are more **noticeable**, **vivid**, or **emotionally striking**, rather than on what is most relevant or statistically significant. This mental model reflects how our attention is naturally drawn to what stands out—whether through colour, intensity, novelty, or drama—often at the expense of more important but less eye-catching factors.

Salience Bias is deeply rooted in human psychology and evolutionary biology. Our ancestors' survival depended on detecting immediate, attention-grabbing stimuli—such as predators, food sources, or social threats. Today, however, this same mechanism can distort our judgment in media, decision-making, and perception.

Example

Consider how people perceive air travel versus car travel. Plane crashes are highly publicized, dramatic, and emotionally charged events. As a result, many people fear flying more than driving—even though statistically, air travel is far safer. The vivid imagery of plane crashes (news coverage, dramatic headlines) becomes more **salient**, skewing perception and risk assessment.

Why It Works

Salience Bias works because the human brain gives more cognitive weight to striking or emotionally intense stimuli. Vivid information is easier to recall and feels more significant, regardless of its actual importance. Emotionally charged or visually dominant information activates stronger neural pathways, making it more memorable and influential in future decisions.

How It Works

- An event or piece of information stands out due to vividness, novelty, or emotional intensity.

- Attention is drawn to it automatically, often subconsciously.

- This salient feature overshadows more relevant but subtler data.

- Decisions and beliefs are formed or reinforced based on what's most noticeable, not what's most accurate.

Application

Salience Bias is frequently exploited in advertising, media, and politics. Marketers highlight bold features or shocking claims to draw attention, even if they're not central to product quality. News organizations focus on sensational stories, because they generate clicks—even when mundane statistics tell a more important story. In decision-making, leaders must be cautious not to prioritize what feels urgent over what is genuinely important.

Key Insights

- What grabs attention isn't always what matters most.

- Emotionally vivid or extreme examples distort risk perception and memory.

- Countering salience bias requires deliberate focus on context, data, and less obvious variables.

- Awareness of this bias helps prevent manipulation by media and marketing.

Conclusion

Salience Bias reveals how easily our minds are hijacked by what stands out. By recognizing this bias, we can shift our attention from the most noticeable to the most meaningful—leading to clearer thinking and better decisions.

10. Self-Handicapping

Mental Model: Self-Handicapping – A Breakdown

Theory

Self-Handicapping is a psychological defence mechanism where individuals deliberately create obstacles or excuses to protect their self-esteem from potential failure. Rather than risk a poor performance being seen as a true reflection of their ability, they sabotage themselves in advance so they can blame the failure on external factors. This mental model reflects how people prioritize the **preservation of self-image** over genuine success.

The concept was introduced by psychologists Edward Jones and Steven Berglas in the 1970s. It operates primarily in achievement contexts—academics, sports, career—where ego and identity are on the line.

Example

Imagine a student who has an important exam but chooses to go out the night before instead of studying. If they perform poorly, they can say, "I didn't really try," protecting their sense of competence. Conversely, if they perform well despite the handicap, they gain an ego boost— proving their ability under pressure.

Why It Works

Self-handicapping works because it gives people a **psychological safety net**. Failure is painful, especially when it feels like a direct judgment of our worth or intelligence. By introducing an excuse—a lack of preparation, illness, bad timing—the individual can **attribute poor outcomes to something other than a lack of ability**. This preserves self-esteem in the short term.

Additionally, it creates a win-win illusion: if they fail, the excuse takes the blame; if they succeed, it enhances their perceived talent ("I succeeded even under these conditions").

How It Works

- The person anticipates a performance where their competence may be evaluated.

- To avoid ego damage from possible failure, they engage in self-sabotaging behaviour (e.g., procrastination, not preparing, substance use).

- When the outcome arrives, they attribute results to the handicap rather than ability.

- This reduces the psychological impact of failure but also limits growth and learning.

Application
Self-handicapping appears in workplaces, schools, sports, and personal goals. Recognizing it is crucial for coaches, educators, and managers who want to support genuine performance development. Encouraging a **growth mindset**—where failure is seen as part of learning—can help reduce the fear that fuels self-handicapping.

Key Insights

- Self-handicapping trades long-term growth for short-term ego protection.

- It is a sign of fear-based thinking, not laziness.

- Safe environments that reward effort, not just outcome, help reduce it.

- Being honest about effort and expectations fosters accountability and self-improvement.

Conclusion

Self-handicapping is a subtle but powerful way people protect their egos from the discomfort of failure. Understanding and addressing it allows for healthier risk-taking, more authentic effort, and better long-term outcomes.

Economic and Financial Models:

11. Law of One Price

Mental Model: Law of One Price – A Breakdown

Theory

The **Law of One Price** is an economic principle stating that identical goods should sell for the same price in efficient markets when there are no transportation costs, trade barriers, or information asymmetries. In other words, in a perfectly competitive market, arbitrage will ensure that the price of a product is equalized across different locations or markets.

This model is grounded in classical economics and assumes rational actors, free trade, and seamless access to information. It underpins theories of market efficiency and global pricing models and helps explain how arbitrageurs (those who exploit price differences) play a role in aligning prices across markets.

Example

Imagine gold is trading for $2,000 per ounce in London but $2,050 per ounce in New York. Traders will buy gold in London and sell it in New York for a profit. As demand increases in London, the price rises, and as supply increases in New York, the price falls. This arbitrage continues until the prices converge, ideally settling at one price across both markets—demonstrating the Law of One Price.

Why It Works

The Law of One Price works because of **arbitrage**—the practice of exploiting price differences across markets to make a profit. In open, competitive environments, the act of buying low in one market and selling high in another forces prices to move toward equilibrium. As more participants exploit the price difference, the gap disappears. This dynamic ensures pricing consistency and prevents persistent inefficiencies.

How It Works

- Identical goods are priced differently across markets.

- Traders identify the discrepancy and buy the cheaper version while selling the more expensive one.

- This creates upward pressure on prices in the lower-cost market and downward pressure in the higher-cost market.

- The price gap narrows until there's no incentive left to arbitrage.

- Prices reach equilibrium: the "one price."

Application

The Law of One Price is widely used in financial markets, global trade, and digital commerce. It's foundational in

currency exchange rates, **commodity trading**, and **stock market pricing**. Online platforms like Amazon or eBay reflect this principle when identical products are sold globally and prices adjust due to competition and consumer comparison.

Key Insights

- Market efficiency is driven by transparency and mobility.

- Barriers such as tariffs, shipping costs, or lack of information weaken the law's effect.

- Arbitrage plays a key role in stabilizing markets.

- The law doesn't always hold perfectly but serves as a useful benchmark.

Conclusion

The Law of One Price emphasizes how free markets tend toward equilibrium. Understanding it helps investors, businesses, and consumers make sense of pricing behaviour and market fairness in a connected global economy.

12. Giffen Goods

Mental Model: Giffen Goods – A Breakdown

Theory

Giffen Goods are a rare and counterintuitive economic concept in which the demand for a good **increases** as its price **rises**, violating the basic **law of demand**. Named after Scottish economist Sir Robert Giffen, this phenomenon applies to inferior goods—items people consume more of as their income falls—where the **income effect** outweighs the **substitution effect**.

Typically, when the price of a good rises, people substitute it with a cheaper alternative. However, in the case of Giffen Goods, the item is so essential and has so few viable substitutes that when its price increases, the consumer paradoxically buys **more** of it—often because they can no longer afford more expensive alternatives.

Example

A classic (though debated) example involves **staple foods like bread or rice** in low-income populations. Suppose a poor household relies heavily on rice. If the price of rice rises, they can no longer afford meat or vegetables and must allocate more of their income to rice just to meet basic calorie needs. As a result, they end up consuming **more rice**, not less—despite the price increase.

Why It Works

Giffen behaviour works under specific conditions: the good must be inferior, it must constitute a large portion of the consumer's budget, and there must be a lack of close substitutes. In such cases, the **income effect** (how a price change affects real income) dominates the **substitution effect** (switching to another product), leading to increased consumption as prices rise.

How It Works

- The price of a basic staple rises.

- The consumer's real income falls, limiting access to more nutritious or diverse foods.

- Instead of reducing consumption of the staple, the consumer increases it because it's the only affordable option.

- The good now occupies an even larger share of their budget, reinforcing the cycle.

Application

Understanding Giffen Goods is crucial in development economics, welfare policy, and poverty analysis. Misjudging the consumption behaviour of low-income groups can lead to poor policy outcomes. For example, removing a food subsidy on a staple good might not reduce its demand but instead deepen nutritional poverty, as people are forced to consume more of the inferior good.

Key Insights

- Giffen Goods contradict standard demand theory but are driven by real-world poverty dynamics.

- They highlight the importance of context in economic modelling.

- Policymakers must understand both substitution and income effects when designing interventions.

- Giffen behaviour reflects **desperation, not preference**.

Conclusion

Giffen Goods reveal how poverty can distort consumer behaviour in ways that defy conventional logic.
Recognizing this helps economists and policymakers design more empathetic and effective responses to the realities of low-income households.

13. Prisoner's Dilemma (Iterated)

Mental Model: Prisoner's Dilemma – A Breakdown

Theory

The **Prisoner's Dilemma** is a foundational concept in **game theory** that illustrates how two rational individuals might not cooperate, even if it is in their best collective interest to do so. The dilemma shows how self-interest and mistrust can lead to worse outcomes for all involved, especially in scenarios requiring mutual cooperation.

It's called a "dilemma" because each participant faces a tough choice: cooperate and risk being betrayed, or defect and guarantee personal gain at the other's expense. The paradox lies in the fact that while mutual cooperation yields a better outcome collectively, rational individuals acting in their own self-interest tend to choose to defect, leading to suboptimal results for both.

Example

Two suspects are arrested for a crime. They are interrogated separately. If both stay silent (cooperate), they each get 1 year in prison. If one testifies (defects) and the other stays silent, the defector goes free while the other gets 5 years. If both testify (both defect), they each get 3 years. Although the best collective outcome is to stay silent, each prisoner reasons that betraying the other gives them a better personal outcome—so both usually defect and end up worse off.

Why It Works

The Prisoner's Dilemma works because it captures the tension between **short-term personal gain** and **long-term mutual benefit**. Humans, companies, or nations often struggle with trust and assume others will act selfishly. Without mechanisms for accountability or repeated interaction, fear of being exploited overrides the incentive to cooperate.

How It Works

- Two or more parties must make a decision without knowing the other's choice.

- Each party's best individual outcome comes from defecting.

- However, if all defect, the collective outcome is worse than if all had cooperated.

- The dilemma is strongest when there's no communication or trust between parties.

Application

The Prisoner's Dilemma is widely used to model real-world challenges: arms races, environmental agreements, price wars, and even personal relationships. It's especially relevant in competitive markets and international diplomacy, where mutual restraint benefits all, but individual incentives drive self-serving actions.

Key Insights

- Cooperation often requires trust, communication, or enforcement mechanisms.

- In repeated interactions (iterated games), cooperation becomes more likely.

- Short-term thinking leads to long-term losses.

- The dilemma highlights how rational choices can lead to irrational group outcomes.

Conclusion

The Prisoner's Dilemma reveals how individual rationality can undermine collective well-being. Understanding this mental model can help individuals, organizations, and nations design better systems that promote trust, reciprocity, and long-term collaboration.

14. Zero-Based Thinking

Mental Model: Zero-Based Thinking – A Breakdown

Theory

Zero-Based Thinking (ZBT) is a mental model rooted in decision-making and critical reflection. It involves evaluating current choices or commitments as if you were starting from scratch—without the burden of past decisions, sunk costs, or emotional attachment. The core question of ZBT is:

"Knowing what I now know, would I start this again?"
If the answer is no, it prompts you to rethink, revise, or exit the situation.

Originally applied in budgeting (zero-based budgeting), the idea has been widely adapted to personal development, business strategy, and life choices. It challenges the **status quo bias** and the **sunk cost fallacy**, encouraging rational, forward-focused thinking.

Example

Imagine someone who has spent three years in a job that makes them miserable. They hesitate to leave because they've invested time, energy, and effort. But using zero-based thinking, they ask, "If I hadn't taken this job and was offered it today, knowing what I now know, would I accept it?" If the answer is no, then staying solely because of past investment is irrational. ZBT suggests it's time to reconsider the path.

Why It Works

Zero-Based Thinking works because it helps **detach emotion and ego** from decisions. By mentally resetting to a fresh starting point, you avoid being trapped by inertia or guilt over past investments. It allows you to prioritize **current value and future benefit**, not past effort or pride.

How It Works

- Identify a current situation, project, investment, or relationship.

- Ask the key ZBT question: *"Knowing what I now know, would I start this again?"*

- If the answer is no, explore why you're still involved and whether exiting or adjusting is possible.

- Use the insight to make proactive, rational decisions moving forward.

Application

ZBT is valuable in business, relationships, career choices, projects, and even habits. Companies can apply it to evaluate unproductive initiatives. Individuals can use it to audit personal commitments or routines. It's particularly effective during periods of change or reflection, such as quarterly reviews or life transitions.

Key Insights

- Sunk costs are irrelevant to future decisions.

- Continuing a bad path doesn't redeem past effort.

- The courage to reassess leads to clarity and better alignment.

- ZBT is not about impulsively quitting—it's about conscious, logical evaluation.

Conclusion

Zero-Based Thinking is a powerful mental reset tool. By asking whether you'd begin something again today, you challenge assumptions, shed emotional baggage, and make sharper, more intentional choices for your future.

15. Path of Least Resistance

Mental Model: Path of Least Resistance – A Breakdown

Theory

The **Path of Least Resistance** is a mental model rooted in physics but widely applicable to human behaviour and decision-making. In nature, energy and matter follow the easiest, most efficient route—rivers carve through soft soil, electricity flows through the most conductive material, and animals follow well-trodden trails. Humans often behave the same way: we tend to choose the option that requires the least effort, conflict, or resistance, especially when faced with complexity or decision fatigue.

This model is closely related to **inertia**, **convenience bias**, and **status quo bias**. While the path of least resistance can be efficient, it also carries the risk of **complacency** or missed opportunities for growth, innovation, or change.

Example

Consider a student who always uses Google to research assignments. It's quick, familiar, and easy. But because they rely only on the first few search results, they rarely dive deeper into academic sources or challenge their own views. Their habit represents the path of least resistance—it's efficient but limits depth and critical thinking.

Why It Works

This model works because the human brain is designed to

conserve energy. Our cognitive systems are optimized to minimize effort, especially under stress or time constraints. We favour habits, routines, and shortcuts that require the least friction, even if they aren't optimal. In the short term, this preserves mental resources; in the long term, it can lead to underperformance or stagnation.

How It Works

- When facing a decision, we subconsciously scan for the easiest or most familiar option.

- Emotional, physical, or cognitive resistance pushes us away from more difficult alternatives.

- We follow the smoother route, reinforcing habits or patterns.

- Over time, this becomes automatic, and the harder (often better) path is ignored.

Application

The Path of Least Resistance can be used **constructively** in design, habit formation, and systems thinking. For example, making healthy food more accessible than junk food nudges better choices. In workflow design, simplifying interfaces or reducing unnecessary steps increases adoption and engagement. Leaders can also minimize resistance to change by breaking down complex goals into smaller, low-friction steps.

Key Insights

- People default to ease, not excellence.

- Environment shapes behaviour—make good choices easier.

- Resistance isn't always bad; growth often lies in challenge.

- Simplifying systems helps steer actions in positive directions.

Conclusion

The Path of Least Resistance highlights our tendency to favour ease over effort. By understanding and designing around this instinct, we can either break harmful patterns or leverage it to build better habits, systems, and decisions.

16. Creative Accounting

Mental Model: Creative Accounting – A Breakdown

Theory

Creative Accounting refers to the manipulation of financial records within the bounds of accounting rules, but in a way that misrepresents the true economic reality of a company. It is not outright fraud, but it deliberately obscures or distorts financial statements to present a more favourable image to investors, regulators, or stakeholders. This mental model stems from a broader understanding of how incentives, loopholes, and regulatory frameworks can be gamed without technically breaking the law.

Creative accounting often exploits flexibility in accounting standards, such as revenue recognition timing, off-balance sheet financing, or non-GAAP (Generally Accepted Accounting Principles) metrics to shape perception, manage earnings, or hide risk.

Example

A famous example is **Enron**, which used special purpose entities (SPEs) to hide debt and inflate profits without technically violating accounting rules at the time. The company appeared healthy to investors, despite being financially unstable. When the truth emerged, Enron collapsed—destroying shareholder value and prompting tighter regulation (e.g. Sarbanes-Oxley Act).

Why It Works

Creative accounting works because of **information asymmetry** and the **illusion of precision**. Most investors or stakeholders don't have the time or expertise to dig deep into footnotes or financial subtleties. As long as the company follows formal rules and presents clean reports, trust tends to follow. Executives under pressure to meet earnings targets or boost stock prices may justify these tactics as temporary or harmless.

How It Works

- Management identifies accounting rules that allow discretion.

- Financial data is arranged or timed in a way that flatters results (e.g., delaying expenses, accelerating revenue).

- Complex structures or vague disclosures obscure the full picture.

- External parties—analysts, media, investors—rely on the surface narrative.

- Over time, the disconnect between perception and reality grows, often leading to crisis.

Application

Understanding creative accounting is essential in investing, auditing, corporate governance, and risk management. It teaches caution: numbers may comply with standards but still mislead. Critical analysis of earnings quality, cash flow, and footnotes can reveal hidden red flags. Companies, too, should build cultures of transparency over performance-at-any-cost.

Key Insights

- Legality doesn't guarantee honesty.

- Incentives drive behaviour—especially where there is pressure to "look good."

- Surface metrics can be dressed up; deeper analysis often tells the real story.

- Oversight mechanisms must evolve with financial engineering tactics.

Conclusion

Creative accounting reveals how perception can be shaped without explicit deception. Recognizing it as a mental model builds scepticism, sharpens analysis, and guards against being misled by well-packaged, but hollow, financial storytelling.

17. Velocity of Innovation

Mental Model: Velocity of Innovation – A Breakdown

Theory

Velocity of Innovation refers to the speed at which new ideas, technologies, or improvements are developed, implemented, and iterated upon within an organization or ecosystem. It emphasizes **momentum over perfection**, focusing on how fast a system can learn, adapt, and evolve. The concept originates from the intersection of **agile methodologies**, **lean startup thinking**, and **systems theory**, and is now widely recognized in tech, product development, and competitive strategy.

A higher velocity of innovation doesn't just mean producing more—it means learning faster, responding to change more effectively, and reducing the time between insight and execution. Organizations that can innovate quickly often outperform slower competitors, not because they always get it right the first time, but because they iterate rapidly and continuously improve.

Example

Consider two smartphone companies. Company A launches a new model every two years after extensive R&D. Company B releases updates every year with smaller but more frequent improvements, learning from real user feedback. Over five years, Company B has refined its product through five learning cycles, while Company A has only had two. The faster feedback loop of Company B increases its adaptability, user satisfaction, and market share—demonstrating a higher velocity of innovation.

Why It Works

Velocity of innovation works because it creates a **continuous learning loop**. Rather than aiming for perfection, teams focus on rapid deployment, testing, and refinement. This model aligns with the real world, where conditions shift, customer needs evolve, and early assumptions often prove wrong. Fast iteration allows faster course correction, reducing the cost of mistakes and increasing the chances of discovering what actually works.

How It Works

- Ideas are turned into minimum viable products (MVPs) quickly.

- Feedback is gathered from real-world use, not just internal assumptions.

- The product or system is revised based on data, not opinion.

- Shorter cycles mean faster learning, better risk management, and more innovation momentum.

Application

Velocity of innovation is crucial in software development, startups, R&D teams, and even policy-making. Companies like Amazon, Tesla, and SpaceX thrive not because every idea is perfect, but because they test, iterate, and move faster than their peers. In education, curriculum design and tech implementation also benefit from quick feedback loops and adaptive planning.

Key Insights

- Innovation is as much about speed and adaptability as creativity.

- Fast cycles reduce risk through early failure and learning.

- Perfectionism kills momentum; progress builds insight.

- Speed must be paired with meaningful feedback to be valuable.

Conclusion

The Velocity of Innovation model highlights that success favors those who learn and adapt quickly. It teaches us that in fast-changing environments, the ability to move— and improve—rapidly is more powerful than getting it perfect the first time.

18. Fat-Tailed Distribution

Mental Model: Fat-Tailed Distribution – A Breakdown

Theory

A **Fat-Tailed Distribution** refers to a statistical pattern where extreme events—far from the average—occur **more frequently** than in a standard bell curve (normal distribution). In these distributions, the "tails" of the graph (representing outlier events) are thicker, or "fat," meaning rare but **high-impact outcomes** are significantly more likely than expected under traditional models.

Fat-tailed distributions are often found in **complex systems**, such as financial markets, natural disasters, pandemics, and technological disruption. Unlike normal distributions, which assume that most results cluster tightly around the mean with rare deviations, fat-tailed events defy these expectations—and carry massive consequences.

Example

In financial markets, traditional models assume that stock price movements follow a normal distribution. However, crashes like the 2008 financial crisis or the 1987 Black Monday show that extreme drops happen more often than the models predict. These are fat-tail events: rare in theory, but surprisingly frequent and devastating in practice.

Why It Works

Fat-tailed events are more common in systems that are **interconnected, non-linear, and prone to feedback loops**. Small changes in one area can escalate and create disproportionately large outcomes. Traditional risk models fail to capture this complexity, leaving systems vulnerable. The fat-tailed model works because it accepts that **rare, high-magnitude events are part of the structure**, not exceptions.

How It Works

- A fat-tailed distribution includes a higher probability of outlier events than normal models.

- These outliers can dominate the total effect (e.g., one bad investment wiping out a portfolio).

- Standard deviation becomes less useful, as extreme values skew the average.

- Systems that appear stable can be **fragile** because of underestimated tail risks.

Application

Fat-tailed thinking is essential in **risk management, investing, climate science, cybersecurity**, and **public health**. It prompts the use of **robust systems, fail-safes**, and **stress testing** rather than relying on average-case assumptions. In business strategy, it encourages building for **resilience**, not just efficiency.

For instance, investors like Nassim Taleb emphasize building "antifragile" portfolios that **benefit** from volatility and protect against rare, catastrophic events—because in fat-tailed systems, those events are not just possible, but probable over time.

Key Insights

- Rare events are more likely than we intuitively believe.

- The majority of impact may come from a minority of events (power laws).

- Planning for average outcomes leads to under preparedness.

- Systems should be built to survive (or gain from) the unexpected.

Conclusion

The Fat-Tailed Distribution mental model reminds us that the biggest risks—and opportunities—often lie at the edges. Thinking in fat tails helps us better navigate a world where the improbable happens more often than we think.

19. Efficient Market Hypothesis

Mental Model: Efficient Market Hypothesis – A Breakdown

Theory

The **Efficient Market Hypothesis (EMH)** is a financial theory that suggests asset prices in a market fully reflect all available information at any given time. Developed by economist **Eugene Fama** in the 1960s, EMH posits that it is **impossible to consistently outperform the market** through stock picking or market timing, since any new information that could affect prices is already baked into current valuations.

EMH is categorized into three forms:

1. **Weak form** – All past price information is reflected in current prices.

2. **Semi-strong form** – All publicly available information is reflected in current prices.

3. **Strong form** – All information, both public and private, is reflected in prices.

In each case, the implication is that **markets are rational**, and any attempts to beat them through analysis or prediction are largely futile in the long run.

Example

Imagine a tech company releases a new earnings report

that beats expectations. According to EMH, investors quickly act on this news, buying the stock and driving its price up almost instantly. By the time you, an average investor, hear the news, the opportunity for profit has already been absorbed into the new price. Trying to "get ahead" of the market after public news breaks is like trying to catch a train that has already left.

Why It Works

EMH works under the assumption that markets consist of many rational participants who are constantly analysing, sharing, and acting on information. This constant competition and instant reaction help ensure prices reflect all known data. In efficient markets, **no arbitrage opportunities last long**, because informed investors quickly eliminate them.

How It Works

- New information is released (e.g., earnings, macroeconomic data).

- Investors react, buying or selling assets based on the perceived impact.

- Prices adjust almost immediately to incorporate the new information.

- The market quickly returns to equilibrium, making excess profit difficult.

Application

EMH has major implications in **investing, portfolio**

management, and **financial policy**. It supports **passive investing strategies** like index funds, suggesting that trying to "beat the market" is not only costly but statistically unlikely. It also informs financial regulation and corporate disclosure standards.

Key Insights

- Beating the market consistently is extremely difficult.

- Most professional fund managers underperform the market over time.

- Passive investing often outperforms active management after costs.

- The market can be efficient, but not always rational—behavioural finance challenges EMH in certain contexts.

Conclusion

The Efficient Market Hypothesis encourages humility in investing. By recognizing that markets are hard to outsmart, it pushes individuals toward smarter, cost-effective strategies and reminds us that the price is usually *right*—because it reflects everything we already know.

20. Boomerang Effect

Mental Model: Boomerang Effect – A Breakdown

Theory

The **Boomerang Effect** is a psychological phenomenon where attempts to persuade someone not only fail, but actually **strengthen their opposing viewpoint**. This counterproductive outcome is especially common when messages are perceived as threatening, manipulative, or overly forceful. Instead of shifting attitudes, the message "boomerangs" back—solidifying resistance and reinforcing pre-existing beliefs.

The concept originates from **reactance theory**, developed by psychologist Jack Brehm, which posits that when people sense their **freedom of choice** is being threatened, they experience psychological discomfort (reactance) and are motivated to restore autonomy—even by doing the opposite of what's suggested.

Example

Imagine a public health campaign that uses graphic images to warn teenagers about the dangers of smoking. While some viewers may be deterred, others—especially adolescents who value independence—may interpret the message as patronizing or controlling. Rather than quitting or avoiding smoking, they may smoke more to reassert their autonomy, demonstrating the boomerang effect.

Why It Works
The Boomerang Effect works because humans are inherently protective of their **freedom of thought and action**. When a message feels coercive or challenges deeply held beliefs, it triggers **cognitive dissonance** and defensive reasoning. Instead of processing the message logically, people focus on rejecting the source or counterarguing to protect their identity, values, or autonomy.

How It Works

- A persuasive message is delivered (e.g., "You must stop doing X").

- The recipient perceives a threat to their freedom or self-concept.

- Psychological reactance kicks in, generating resistance.

- The individual may reject the message outright or double down on the opposing belief.

- Instead of persuasion, the opposite effect is achieved.

Application
Understanding the Boomerang Effect is critical in **marketing, public health, education, politics**, and **leadership**. Communicators must consider **tone, autonomy, and audience values** when crafting messages. Effective persuasion involves **inviting engagement**, offering

choices, and framing ideas in non-threatening ways. For example, motivational interviewing in counselling avoids direct commands, instead guiding individuals to discover their own reasons for change.

Key Insights

- Pressure creates resistance; persuasion requires subtlety.

- People are more open to change when they feel in control.

- Effective communication respects autonomy and avoids shaming.

- Overly aggressive messaging can entrench the very behaviour it aims to stop.

Conclusion

The Boomerang Effect highlights how persuasion can backfire when not delivered thoughtfully. Recognizing this mental model helps us craft messages that **invite reflection rather than resistance**, building trust and fostering genuine change through respect and empathy.

Systems and Physics Models:

21. Critical Point

Mental Model: Critical Point – A Breakdown

Theory
A **Critical Point** refers to a threshold or tipping point within a system where a **small input causes a disproportionate, often irreversible change**. Borrowed from thermodynamics and physics (e.g., the point at which water becomes vapor), this concept applies broadly to systems thinking, economics, environmental science, behaviour change, and social dynamics. A critical point represents the moment a system shifts from one state to another—often suddenly and nonlinearly.

In complex systems, critical points are **inflection moments**: before the point, the system appears stable; after it, transformation accelerates. Recognizing these points is essential for anticipating cascading effects, preventing collapse, or catalysing breakthrough change.

Example
Consider the global climate system. As Arctic ice melts, less sunlight is reflected (the albedo effect weakens), warming the Earth further. At a certain **critical point**, this feedback loop becomes self-reinforcing, pushing the climate into a new, hotter state. Passing that threshold means damage accelerates rapidly and is much harder to reverse.

Why It Works

Critical points work because complex systems are often **nonlinear**, meaning the relationship between cause and effect isn't proportional. Inputs accumulate until a hidden threshold is reached. Then, the system rapidly reconfigures itself, moving into a new equilibrium. People often underestimate these points because everything seems stable—until it isn't.

How It Works

- A system absorbs stress, change, or pressure gradually.

- No immediate, visible changes occur—feedback seems manageable.

- At the critical point, even a minor input (a spark, idea, or failure) triggers a rapid transformation.

- After the point is passed, change is often self-sustaining or irreversible.

Application

The critical point model is vital in **economics** (market crashes), **public health** (disease outbreaks), **social movements** (viral trends or protests), and **engineering** (load-bearing structures). In innovation, a product may gain slow adoption—until reaching a tipping point where usage surges. In leadership or policy, applying consistent effort over time may appear fruitless until a breakthrough is suddenly reached.

Key Insights

- Systems often change slowly—until they change fast.

- Monitoring thresholds is more important than observing averages.

- Preventive action is most effective before the critical point, not after.

- Recognizing leading indicators can help manage or harness disruption.

Conclusion

The Critical Point mental model teaches us that **big changes often follow seemingly small events**—if conditions are right. Whether preventing breakdown or triggering progress, understanding when systems are near tipping points empowers better decisions, timing, and strategy.

22. Diffusion of Innovations

Mental Model: Diffusion of Innovations – A Breakdown

Theory

The **Diffusion of Innovations** is a sociological model developed by **Everett Rogers** that explains how, why, and at what rate new ideas, products, or technologies spread through a population. It categorizes adopters into five groups: **Innovators**, **Early Adopters**, **Early Majority**, **Late Majority**, and **Laggards**—each with distinct attitudes toward risk, change, and social influence.

The theory suggests that adoption is not random but follows a predictable curve: at first, uptake is slow, led by risk-takers. Then, if a critical mass is reached, momentum builds rapidly as the majority follows suit. The process is influenced by factors like communication channels, social systems, perceived advantage, and cultural readiness.

Example

Consider the adoption of smartphones. Initially, only tech enthusiasts and early adopters used them. As their utility became clear (e.g., apps, cameras, internet access), a tipping point was reached. The early and late majority joined in, turning smartphones into a near-universal technology. Laggards followed much later, often out of necessity rather than choice.

Why It Works

The model works because human behaviour is shaped by **social proof, perceived value**, and **network effects**. Most people prefer to wait and see if an innovation is successful or useful before adopting it. As more people adopt, the perceived risk decreases and the incentive to join increases. This creates a self-reinforcing cycle, especially once a **critical mass** (typically around 15–18% adoption) is achieved.

How It Works

- Innovators take the initial risk.

- Early adopters follow, validating the idea.

- Early majority waits for evidence and endorsement.

- Late majority joins when the innovation becomes standard or expected.

- Laggards resist change until forced by necessity or obsolescence.

- Adoption accelerates as social, economic, and technological infrastructure supports the innovation.

Application

This model is crucial in **marketing, product development, policymaking, education**, and **healthcare**. Companies use it to tailor strategies for each adopter group—targeting innovators with cutting-edge features and later groups with reliability and social proof. Governments apply it in promoting new practices, like renewable energy or vaccination campaigns, by identifying influencers and barriers to adoption.

Key Insights

- Adoption follows a curve—different groups require different messaging.

- Crossing the "chasm" between early adopters and the early majority is often the hardest step.

- Timing, trust, and visibility are critical in spreading new ideas.

- Innovations that meet real needs, are easy to use, and show visible benefits diffuse faster.

Conclusion

The Diffusion of Innovations model helps us understand **how change spreads**, how to influence adoption, and how to overcome resistance. By recognizing where people are on the adoption curve, we can craft smarter strategies to accelerate meaningful innovation.

23. Tipping Point

Mental Model: Tipping Point – A Breakdown

Theory

A **Tipping Point** refers to the critical threshold at which a small change causes a larger, often irreversible shift in a system, behaviour, or trend. Coined and popularized in social science and systems thinking, especially by **Malcolm Gladwell** in his book *The Tipping Point*, this model explains how phenomena—such as ideas, behaviours, or products—can suddenly gain massive momentum after crossing a certain adoption or influence threshold.

Before the tipping point, growth is slow and effortful. After it, the system becomes self-propelling, like a domino effect or chain reaction. This principle is found across domains: biology, economics, epidemiology, technology, and culture.

Example

Social media adoption illustrates this well. Facebook started with slow growth on college campuses. Once a critical mass of users signed up, it reached a tipping point. Suddenly, network effects kicked in: more users made it more valuable, which attracted even more users. What had been a niche tool rapidly became a global social platform.

Why It Works

The Tipping Point works because systems often exhibit **nonlinear behaviour**. A small, well-timed input—when the system is ripe—can yield exponential results. People and systems resist change until a certain pressure or influence accumulates, at which point the path of least resistance flips toward adoption, behaviour change, or systemic shift.

This also ties to **social proof**: when enough people adopt or believe something, others are much more likely to follow, especially those previously on the fence.

How It Works

- Early adopters or influencers seed an idea, behaviour, or trend.

- Gradual change builds beneath the surface—often unnoticed.

- Key thresholds (e.g., market share, opinion change, viral spread) are crossed.

- Momentum builds rapidly, triggering large-scale, self-sustaining growth or change.

- After the tipping point, reversal becomes difficult or impossible.

Application

This model is essential in **marketing, epidemiology, environmental science, policy**, and **innovation strategy**. For instance, marketers use influencers to push a product toward a tipping point of awareness. In public health, understanding the tipping point of infection spread helps design better interventions. In climate science, avoiding environmental tipping points is crucial to long-term stability.

Key Insights

- Big change often hinges on small, timely pushes.

- Systems can appear stable—until they suddenly aren't.

- Early momentum is critical, but strategic targeting of key influencers or leverage points accelerates adoption.

- Once past the tipping point, feedback loops drive further acceleration.

Conclusion

The Tipping Point model emphasizes the power of timing, network effects, and critical mass. It shows how small actions, placed correctly, can ignite major transformations—making it a vital tool for change-makers, strategists, and leaders.

24. Bottleneck Effect

Mental Model: Bottleneck Effect – A Breakdown

Theory

The **Bottleneck Effect** is a systems-based mental model that describes how the **slowest or most constrained part of a system** determines the speed, efficiency, or capacity of the entire system. Just like the narrow neck of a bottle controls how fast liquid can flow out, a single limiting factor can cap performance, regardless of how optimized other parts are.

This concept is widely used in **operations management**, **engineering**, **project planning**, and **biology**. It emphasizes that improving overall performance requires identifying and alleviating the true constraint—not just optimizing every component indiscriminately.

Example

Consider a factory with five workstations on an assembly line. If four stations can each process 100 units per hour, but the fifth can only handle 60 units per hour, the **entire system's output** is limited to 60 units per hour. No matter how fast the other stations are, they will be forced to wait, build up excess inventory, or waste resources—all due to a single bottleneck.

Why It Works

The Bottleneck Effect works because **systems are**

interconnected. The output of one part is often the input for another. A bottleneck creates a **cascading delay**, limiting throughput and increasing inefficiencies like wait times, inventory buildup, or cost. Focusing on the constraint—rather than every part of the system— produces the most significant gains.

This idea is central to **The Theory of Constraints**, which teaches that the **weakest link determines the strength of the whole chain**.

How It Works

- The system is analysed for flow of information, resources, or processes.

- A limiting step (bottleneck) is identified as the slowest or most capacity-restricted point.

- All upstream efforts accumulate at the bottleneck, and downstream functions are underutilized.

- Until the bottleneck is addressed, the system cannot improve meaningfully.

- Once relieved, a new bottleneck may emerge, requiring iterative improvement.

Application

This model applies across fields: in **project management**, it helps teams identify the person or step delaying the workflow; in **traffic systems**, it explains congestion points; in **software development**, it highlights coding or deployment delays. Even in personal productivity, tasks like checking email too often can become a bottleneck in deep work.

Key Insights

- Don't optimize everything—optimize the constraint.

- Bottlenecks are often hidden; focus on throughput, not activity.

- Removing one bottleneck usually reveals the next— continuous improvement is essential.

- Addressing the constraint can deliver exponential gains in efficiency and effectiveness.

Conclusion

The Bottleneck Effect teaches that improving a system means focusing not on what's working fastest, but on **what's holding everything back**. By identifying and addressing constraints, we unlock greater flow, productivity, and performance with fewer wasted resources.

25. Convergence

Mental Model: Convergence – A Breakdown

Theory

Convergence is a mental model that describes how diverse elements—ideas, technologies, trends, or disciplines— gradually come together over time to produce a **unified outcome** or a **significant breakthrough**. The convergence model suggests that **innovation**, **progress**, or **clarity** often emerges not from a single source, but from the intersection of multiple lines of development that begin separately but move toward common ground.

This model is rooted in **systems thinking**, **technological innovation**, and **evolutionary biology**, where unrelated paths gradually align due to shared pressures, mutual benefit, or systemic compatibility.

Example

A powerful example is the **smartphone**. It wasn't a sudden invention, but the result of convergence: computing power, wireless communication, touchscreens, miniaturization, battery life, and software design all evolved independently. Once they reached a certain maturity, these separate technologies converged to create the modern smartphone—a product that changed the world.

Why It Works

Convergence works because **complex systems evolve in parallel**, often without coordination. When multiple technologies, ideas, or movements advance simultaneously, the probability increases that their combined application will lead to **nonlinear outcomes**. Each component may seem limited alone, but when aligned, they unlock new possibilities.

From a cognitive standpoint, convergence mirrors **pattern recognition**—our brain's natural tendency to connect disparate information into a meaningful whole. It also explains how innovation accelerates once the "pieces of the puzzle" fall into place.

How It Works

- Multiple disciplines, tools, or ideas evolve independently.

- Each follows its own trajectory, improving incrementally.

- Over time, points of synergy appear—shared platforms, problems, or opportunities.

- When the parts align, they enable a transformative outcome greater than the sum of the inputs.

Application

This model applies to **innovation strategy, career planning, creative problem-solving**, and **trend forecasting**. In business, companies that anticipate convergence can seize new markets (e.g., Tesla combining battery tech, software, and auto manufacturing). In personal development, skills like coding, design, and storytelling may converge into new roles like UX design or content engineering. Educators and strategists can use this model to predict how disciplines may overlap and guide interdisciplinary thinking.

Key Insights

- True innovation often emerges from intersection, not isolation.

- Seemingly unrelated progress can suddenly become crucial when convergence occurs.

- Investing early in parallel areas increases readiness when they align.

- Convergence often marks the transition from linear to exponential growth.

Conclusion

The Convergence mental model teaches us to watch the edges—where ideas and technologies begin to overlap. By anticipating and embracing these intersections, we position ourselves to recognize or create transformative breakthroughs that others might miss.

26. Emergence

Mental Model: Emergence – A Breakdown

Theory

Emergence is a phenomenon in which complex patterns, behaviours, or properties arise from the interactions of simpler components—**without any central control**. The key idea is that the **whole becomes greater than the sum of its parts**, and that the final outcome often cannot be predicted just by analysing the individual components.

Emergence is fundamental to **systems thinking, complexity science**, and **network theory**. It explains how decentralized or unintelligent parts, when interacting according to simple rules, can produce highly organized and intelligent outcomes at the system level.

Example

A classic example is an **ant colony**. Individually, ants are simple creatures that follow basic rules—like following pheromone trails or avoiding obstacles. Yet collectively, they build intricate nests, find optimal food routes, and adapt to environmental changes. No single ant understands the system, but through local interactions, intelligent behaviour *emerges* at the colony level.

Why It Works

Emergence works because **interactions between parts lead to feedback loops** and **self-organization**. These feedback loops amplify certain behaviours while dampening others, guiding the system toward patterns, efficiencies, or adaptations that weren't explicitly programmed or intended. This allows for resilience, flexibility, and adaptation in dynamic environments—traits central to both biological and social systems.

How It Works

- Simple agents operate based on local rules or inputs.

- They interact with each other and their environment.

- Over time, patterns form through repetition, feedback, and reinforcement.

- A larger, coherent structure or behaviour emerges—often unpredictable from individual actions alone.

Application

Emergence has applications in **technology**, **economics**, **biology**, **urban planning**, and **organizational behaviour**. In software, algorithms inspired by emergence (e.g. swarm intelligence) solve complex optimization problems. In markets, individual buyers and sellers create price systems without a central planner. In teams, culture or innovation can emerge organically through open collaboration rather than top-down mandates.

For leaders, the key is to design environments where **positive emergent behaviour** is encouraged—by setting rules, fostering communication, and allowing distributed decision-making.

Key Insights

- Complex results don't require complex instructions.

- Top-down control is often less effective than enabling bottom-up interaction.

- Small actions, when multiplied across a system, can lead to large-scale change.

- Emergent systems can be more adaptive, resilient, and innovative.

Conclusion

The Emergence mental model shows us that powerful outcomes can arise from simple rules and interactions. By shifting focus from controlling parts to enabling patterns, we unlock the hidden potential of complex systems— whether in nature, technology, or human collaboration.

27. Kinetic Energy of Ideas

Mental Model: Kinetic Energy of Ideas – A Breakdown

Theory
The **Kinetic Energy of Ideas** is a metaphorical mental model that views ideas not as static concepts, but as **dynamic forces** capable of movement, momentum, and impact—much like kinetic energy in physics. In this model, the value of an idea isn't just in its brilliance, but in its **motion**: how far it spreads, how deeply it resonates, and what actions it sparks.

Just as kinetic energy in physics depends on **mass** and **velocity**, the "energy" of an idea depends on its **substance** (relevance, clarity, truth) and its **momentum** (how rapidly and widely it's communicated or adopted). This model emphasizes that ideas gain power through dissemination, discussion, and iteration.

Example
Consider the idea of **"remote work"**. Before 2020, it was a fringe notion in many industries. But during the COVID-19 pandemic, the idea gained momentum. As more companies adopted it, its kinetic energy surged—spreading across sectors, influencing real estate, technology, policy, and culture. The idea moved from a niche concept to a

global shift, demonstrating how an idea in motion can change systems.

Why It Works

The model works because **ideas only create impact when acted upon or shared**. A brilliant idea locked in someone's mind has potential energy but no influence. When it's expressed, debated, applied, and spread, it accumulates kinetic energy—driving change and innovation. Additionally, **network effects** amplify the spread and transformation of ideas, turning small sparks into widespread movements.

How It Works

- An idea is conceived (potential energy).

- It is shared through speech, writing, or design.

- If it resonates, others adopt, adapt, and share it further.

- Momentum builds through visibility, relevance, and repetition.

- The idea becomes a force—shaping decisions, products, or social change.

Application

This model is crucial in **entrepreneurship**, **marketing**, **education**, and **leadership**. Founders need to get their ideas moving—pitching, iterating, and testing. Teachers use narratives and analogies to move concepts into students' minds. Movements and campaigns rely on virality, clarity, and emotional resonance to convert static beliefs into action.

Key Insights

- An idea's power lies in its motion, not just its merit.

- Velocity (how fast it's shared) and mass (how much it matters) drive influence.

- Clarity, storytelling, and timing increase an idea's energy.

- Dormant ideas need catalysts—people, platforms, or moments—to activate them.

Conclusion

The Kinetic Energy of Ideas reminds us that the **true power of thinking is in doing and sharing**. By propelling ideas into motion, we transform passive thought into active change— turning insight into innovation, and knowledge into momentum.

28. Structural Hole

Mental Model: Structural Hole – A Breakdown

Theory

The **Structural Hole** theory, developed by sociologist **Ronald Burt**, refers to the gap between two groups or individuals in a social network who are **not directly connected**, despite having potential mutual interests or knowledge. A structural hole represents an opportunity. Those who **bridge** this gap—known as **brokers**—gain a powerful strategic advantage by accessing **non-redundant information** and facilitating connections others can't.

The value of this model lies in the **network position** rather than status or resources. People who act as connectors between otherwise isolated clusters become indispensable conduits of innovation, influence, and insight.

Example

Consider someone working in both tech and healthcare sectors. These industries often operate in silos. A professional who understands both worlds and can connect developers with clinicians bridges a structural hole. They can spot opportunities others miss—like developing a digital health app—simply because they access information across domains that don't naturally talk to each other.

Why It Works

The model works because most networks are **highly clustered**—people tend to interact within their own circles. This leads to **redundant information**, where everyone shares similar knowledge. Brokers who span structural holes gain **unique access** to diverse perspectives, tools, or markets. They become **more innovative, influential**, and often more valuable to their organizations.

Structural holes also create **control advantages**: brokers can shape how and when information is shared, influencing decisions and dynamics across groups.

How It Works

- A network contains clusters of connected individuals or groups.

- Between these clusters, gaps (structural holes) often exist.

- A person who bridges the gap links otherwise unconnected parties.

- They access diverse, novel information and control the flow between groups.

- Over time, they become seen as innovators, problem-solvers, and leaders.

Application

Structural holes are a powerful concept in **career growth, innovation, entrepreneurship**, and **organizational strategy**. Startups often disrupt industries by connecting unlinked markets or ideas. Within organizations, cross-functional leaders who understand and connect different departments are often the most impactful. For individuals, cultivating relationships across fields or cultures expands one's influence and opportunity.

Key Insights

- Opportunity often lies in the space between disciplines or communities.

- Bridging silos creates value through insight, not just knowledge.

- Diverse networks drive innovation and career mobility.

- You don't need to be an expert everywhere—just the connector between experts.

Conclusion

The Structural Hole mental model shows that value often lies in the **gaps between groups, not within them.** Those who build bridges—across industries, ideas, or people—can unlock powerful leverage, becoming indispensable agents of connection, creativity, and change.

29. Information Asymmetry

Mental Model: Information Asymmetry – A Breakdown

Theory

Information Asymmetry refers to a situation where one party in a transaction or interaction has **more or better information** than the other. This imbalance can lead to **inefficiencies, manipulation, mistrust**, or **market failure**, depending on the context. The concept was formalized by economist **George Akerlof** in his influential paper *The Market for Lemons* (1970), which explored how used car markets often suffer because buyers can't distinguish between good and bad cars.

Information asymmetry is a core concept in **economics, negotiation, finance**, and **ethics**, and it challenges the assumption that markets are always efficient. It suggests that transparency and incentives play a crucial role in maintaining fairness and trust.

Example

Consider the health insurance industry. Insurers don't know as much about the health risks of potential clients as the clients do themselves. A person with a chronic illness is more likely to seek insurance, leading to a pool of high-risk individuals. This is a form of **adverse selection**, where the lack of information on one side results in skewed outcomes, higher premiums, or insurers exiting the market.

Why It Works

Information asymmetry works because **knowledge is power**—the party with more information can make better decisions, predict outcomes more accurately, and exploit their advantage. The imbalance affects **trust**, increases **risk**, and distorts **market behaviour**. It also underlines the importance of **signalling** (providing credible information) and **screening** (extracting hidden information) as mechanisms to reduce uncertainty.

How It Works

- One party holds more or better information than the other.

- This party can exploit their position by hiding, distorting, or leveraging the information.

- The less-informed party faces higher uncertainty and risk.

- As a result, transactions may be avoided, priced unfairly, or misjudged.

- Over time, mistrust and inefficiency increase unless corrective mechanisms are introduced.

Application

Information asymmetry is a critical consideration in **contract law, investing, hiring, sales**, and **policy design**. Regulatory frameworks like **disclosure requirements,**

auditing standards, and **consumer protection laws** are often designed to reduce information imbalances. In business, transparency, reputation, and third-party verification (like reviews or certifications) are essential tools for levelling the informational playing field.

Key Insights

- The less informed party often bears the greater risk.

- Reducing information gaps builds trust and stability.

- Asymmetry can be exploited—but often unsustainably.

- Systems function better when incentives align and information flows freely.

Conclusion

Information Asymmetry reminds us that **fairness and efficiency depend on transparency**. By recognizing and correcting these imbalances, we create systems—markets, teams, relationships—that are more stable, ethical, and effective.

30. Punctuated Equilibrium

Mental Model: Punctuated Equilibrium – A Breakdown

Theory

Punctuated Equilibrium is a theory originally proposed in **evolutionary biology** by **Stephen Jay Gould** and **Niles Eldredge**. It suggests that evolution doesn't happen gradually over time, as once believed, but rather through **long periods of stability (equilibrium)** interrupted by **short, intense bursts of rapid change** (punctuations).

Though rooted in biology, this model has since been applied across disciplines—including economics, politics, technology, and organizational behaviour—to explain how systems often experience sudden, transformative change after extended periods of little to no movement. It challenges the linear "slow and steady" model of progress by acknowledging the role of thresholds, catalysts, and system-level shifts.

Example

A real-world example is the **technology industry**. For years, the mobile phone evolved incrementally—slightly better buttons, battery life, and screens. Then the release of the **iPhone in 2007** acted as a punctuation event, rapidly transforming the industry. It combined a touchscreen, apps, and internet connectivity into one device, triggering a new technological and social era. The shift was abrupt, reshaping consumer behaviour and business models in a very short time.

Why It Works
Punctuated Equilibrium works because **systems tend to resist change** due to inertia, path dependence, and structural rigidity. However, **stress builds over time**— through accumulating inefficiencies, external shocks, or emerging innovations. Eventually, a tipping point is reached, forcing rapid adaptation or collapse. These bursts often seem sudden but are the result of unseen pressure or opportunity gathering beneath the surface.

How It Works

- A system remains in a stable state, appearing resistant to change.

- Pressure accumulates silently (e.g. new technologies, social unrest, market inefficiencies).

- A triggering event (internal or external) breaks the equilibrium.

- Rapid transformation follows as the system reorganizes to a new state.

- A new period of relative stability emerges—until the next punctuation.

Application
This model is valuable in **leadership, change management, innovation, public policy, and personal growth**.
Understanding it can help leaders anticipate resistance

during stable periods while preparing for rapid change. It also highlights the importance of **recognizing inflection points** and being agile enough to respond when they arise.

Key Insights

- Change is often nonlinear—nothing happens for a long time, then everything changes quickly.

- Stability isn't stagnation—it can be preparation.

- Most systems are more fragile or dynamic than they appear.

- Transformative change is usually preceded by invisible buildup.

Conclusion

Punctuated Equilibrium teaches us that **progress isn't always smooth or predictable**. By watching for pressure points and staying adaptable, we can navigate sudden shifts more effectively and seize opportunities during disruption.

Social and Psychological Models:

31. Tribalism

Mental Model: Tribalism – A Breakdown

Theory

Tribalism is a mental model that describes the human tendency to form **strong in-groups** and define ourselves in opposition to **out-groups**. Rooted in our evolutionary history, tribalism was once a survival mechanism: being part of a group meant safety, cooperation, and shared resources. Over time, this instinct evolved into a deep-seated psychological bias toward loyalty, identity, and conformity within one's group—be it cultural, political, religious, or professional.

This model helps explain why humans often show **favouritism** toward those like them and **distrust or demonize** outsiders, even when such divisions are artificial. It highlights how group identity can override logic, individual beliefs, or objective reasoning in favour of collective loyalty.

Example

A modern example is **political polarization**. People often adopt extreme stances not because of careful analysis, but because "their side" supports it. Even when presented with evidence that contradicts their position, individuals may double down to protect their group identity. The need to belong outweighs the need to be correct.

Why It Works

Tribalism works because it taps into our **emotional wiring**. Belonging to a group satisfies basic human needs—security, significance, identity, and purpose. In uncertain environments, aligning with a group reduces cognitive load: instead of evaluating every issue independently, we adopt group norms and values. Emotionally, we are wired to seek **social cohesion**, and conformity provides psychological safety.

How It Works

- Individuals affiliate with a group based on shared values, identity, or interests.

- Group cohesion is reinforced through symbols, language, and rituals.

- In-group loyalty strengthens, while out-group hostility increases.

- Dissent is discouraged, and conformity is rewarded.

- Rationality often yields to emotional loyalty and groupthink.

Application

Understanding tribalism is essential in **leadership, marketing, conflict resolution, politics**, and **social media dynamics**. Leaders can foster healthy group identity without promoting division. Marketers can craft messages that resonate with group values. Conflict mediators must navigate tribal narratives to find common ground. And in digital spaces, awareness of tribalism can reduce misinformation and polarization.

Key Insights

- Belonging often trumps accuracy or logic.

- Tribalism simplifies complexity, but at a cost: division, bias, and echo chambers.

- Recognizing tribal behaviour in ourselves and others enables more empathetic, critical thinking.

- Tribal energy can be channelled constructively— toward shared goals rather than rigid divides.

Conclusion

The Tribalism mental model reminds us that beneath our modern lives, we're still wired for belonging. While tribes provide strength and identity, unchecked tribalism can blind us to truth and deepen divides. Recognizing its pull helps us engage more thoughtfully, lead more wisely, and build bridges instead of walls.

32. Pratfall Effect

Mental Model: Pratfall Effect – A Breakdown

Theory

The **Pratfall Effect** is a psychological phenomenon where a **highly competent person becomes more likable** after making a small, relatable mistake. The term comes from social psychology research by **Elliot Aronson** in the 1960s, who found that people admired experts more when they showed slight human flaws—such as spilling coffee or stumbling over a word—compared to when they appeared perfect.

The theory challenges the common belief that perfection attracts admiration. In reality, **flaws can humanize people**, especially when competence is already established. The key is the balance: the mistake must be minor and non-threatening, and the person must first be seen as capable.

Example

Imagine a confident and charismatic public speaker delivering a polished presentation. Near the end, they drop their notes, laugh it off, and carry on. Rather than losing credibility, they often become more relatable and endearing. The small error signals authenticity, making the speaker more approachable and trustworthy without undermining their skill.

Why It Works

The Pratfall Effect works because **perfection can create psychological distance**. People may admire someone flawless, but they struggle to connect with them. A small error reveals vulnerability, which triggers empathy and familiarity. It reassures the audience that the person is **"human like me"**, reducing feelings of intimidation or inferiority.

Importantly, the effect **only enhances likability when competence is already assumed**. If the individual is average or unproven, a mistake may simply reinforce doubts about their ability.

How It Works

- A person demonstrates competence or authority.

- They commit a harmless blunder (a pratfall).

- Observers' perceptions shift slightly—from admiration to affection.

- The mistake adds relatability, enhancing interpersonal appeal.

- This increased likability can improve persuasion, trust, and social connection.

Application

This model is useful in **public speaking, leadership, branding, interviews**, and **media presence**. Leaders who admit to small errors or show humility often earn more loyalty than those who project perfection. Brands that acknowledge past missteps (with transparency and improvement) can build deeper customer trust. Creators and influencers who reveal behind-the-scenes struggles often foster stronger community engagement.

Key Insights

- Flaws can strengthen, not weaken, connection— when framed correctly.

- Competence must come first; relatability follows.

- Vulnerability, authenticity, and humour enhance trust and likability.

- Over-polished perfection can alienate rather than inspire.

Conclusion

The Pratfall Effect teaches that **being human makes you more persuasive and relatable**. A small stumble, in the right context, can break down barriers, build trust, and turn admiration into genuine connection.

33. Group Polarization

Mental Model: Group Polarization – A Breakdown

Theory

Group Polarization is a social psychology phenomenon where individuals, after engaging in group discussion, tend to adopt **more extreme positions** than they initially held. Rather than moderating opinions, group interaction often amplifies the dominant viewpoint, pushing members toward **greater intensity**—either more risk-seeking or more conservative, depending on the group's initial lean.

This model was first studied in the 1960s and is closely related to **confirmation bias**, **social identity theory**, and **echo chambers**. It shows how being part of a group doesn't just reinforce our views—it can **intensify** them.

Example

Consider a group of investors mildly optimistic about a tech stock. After discussing the company's growth potential, market buzz, and analyst reports, the group becomes **extremely bullish**, convincing each other that the stock is a "sure bet." Their post-discussion decisions may involve riskier investments than any individual would have taken alone—demonstrating group polarization in action.

Why It Works

Group polarization works because of two key forces:

1. **Social comparison** – People want to fit in or appear "correct" within the group. When they see others lean in one direction, they adjust their stance slightly further in the same direction to gain approval.

2. **Persuasive arguments** – In groups, individuals are exposed to new supporting points for their initial view, making that view seem even more robust. More arguments = more confidence.

This combination reinforces beliefs, increases certainty, and leads to more extreme attitudes or decisions.

How It Works

- Individuals enter a discussion with mild or moderate opinions.

- Through conversation, they hear arguments that support and extend their view.

- Social validation encourages further alignment with the dominant group stance.

- Dissenting voices, if present, are often marginalized or self-silenced.

- The group exits with more polarized, often overconfident, views.

Application

Group polarization is critical in **politics, corporate decision-making, social media, legal settings**, and **activism**. Online platforms and algorithm-driven content often create "filter bubbles" that intensify polarization. In boardrooms or juries, lack of diverse viewpoints can lead to extreme or poor decisions. Awareness of this model helps in designing better group dynamics, encouraging critical thinking, and fostering dissent.

Key Insights

- Group discussion doesn't always lead to better reasoning—it can entrench bias.

- Diversity of opinion is a safeguard against polarization.

- Leaders must create space for dissent and balance.

- Social dynamics often overpower individual rationality.

Conclusion

Group Polarization reveals how collective environments can magnify opinions and behaviour. Recognizing this effect helps individuals and organizations make **more balanced, thoughtful decisions**—especially when stakes are high and consensus feels too easy.

34. Bandwagon Effect

Mental Model: Bandwagon Effect – A Breakdown

Theory

The **Bandwagon Effect** is a cognitive bias and social phenomenon where individuals adopt certain behaviours, beliefs, or trends simply because they see others doing the same. Rather than evaluating ideas based on their intrinsic merit, people often follow the crowd—assuming that if many believe or do something, it must be right or beneficial.

This mental model is rooted in **herd behaviour, social proof**, and the **desire for belonging**. First studied in political science and psychology, it shows how group momentum can override critical thinking, especially in uncertain or high-pressure environments. The name originates from 19th-century political campaigns where candidates would ride on literal bandwagons, and crowds would join simply because others were cheering.

Example

A common example is seen in financial markets. During a speculative bubble, people buy assets not because of solid fundamentals, but because "everyone else is buying." Take the rise of certain cryptocurrencies or meme stocks—many investors jumped in late, driven by hype, viral content, or fear of missing out (FOMO). When prices collapsed, those following the crowd—without due diligence—faced losses.

Why It Works

The Bandwagon Effect works because humans are **social creatures** who seek validation, fear exclusion, and rely on shortcuts in decision-making. In uncertain or ambiguous situations, looking to the majority is an efficient way to decide. Emotionally, it feels safer to go along with the group than to stand out and risk being wrong or alone.

This effect is amplified by modern media and technology, where trends can spread rapidly and virally, giving the illusion of universal acceptance or truth.

How It Works

- An idea, product, or behaviour gains initial popularity.

- As more people adopt it, social visibility and credibility increase.

- Observers infer legitimacy from popularity and follow suit.

- Momentum builds, creating a feedback loop of increasing adoption.

- Eventually, people join not for value, but because others are already involved.

Application

The Bandwagon Effect is vital in **marketing, politics, social**

media, investing, fashion, and **public opinion formation**. Marketers use tactics like testimonials, influencer endorsements, or visible popularity metrics (e.g., likes, shares) to trigger this effect. Political campaigns benefit from showing rising poll numbers or packed rallies to signal growing support.

Key Insights

- Popularity is not always a proxy for truth or value.

- Herd behaviour can override rational thought, especially in high-emotion contexts.

- Trend participation may lead to regret if driven by external pressure, not personal conviction.

- Critical thinking and delayed judgment help resist bandwagon pressure.

Conclusion

The Bandwagon Effect reveals how easily social influence can shape behaviour and belief. By recognizing this mental model, individuals and organizations can make more **informed, independent decisions**—and avoid being swept up by the crowd without questioning why.

35. Wisdom of the Crowd

Mental Model: Wisdom of the Crowd – A Breakdown

Theory
The **Wisdom of the Crowd** is the idea that large groups of diverse, independently-thinking individuals can collectively make **better decisions or predictions** than even experts. When certain conditions are met, the aggregated input of many people often outperforms the judgment of a few.

This concept was famously introduced by **Francis Galton** in the early 1900s. At a livestock fair, he observed that the average of hundreds of people's guesses about an ox's weight was more accurate than any individual estimate— including those made by farmers and butchers. This insight sparked widespread interest in crowd-based intelligence, which is now central to fields like **crowdsourcing**, **prediction markets**, and **collective decision-making**.

Example
A modern example is **Wikipedia**. Rather than being written by a small panel of experts, its content is produced and edited by a vast global community. Despite concerns about open editing, studies have shown that the accuracy of popular Wikipedia entries often rivals that of traditional encyclopaedias—thanks to the scale, diversity, and independence of its contributors.

Why It Works

The Wisdom of the Crowd works because **diversity of thought cancels out individual biases**. When people approach a question from different backgrounds and perspectives, their errors tend to be uncorrelated. When averaged, these errors diminish, and the collective insight becomes surprisingly accurate. This model also thrives on **decentralization**, avoiding the pitfalls of groupthink or central authority errors.

How It Works

- Each individual provides an independent judgment or estimate.

- These inputs are aggregated (averaged, voted on, etc.).

- Outliers and biases cancel each other out.

- The result reflects a more balanced and accurate answer than most single inputs.

Application

This model is used in **prediction markets, crowdsourced design, consumer feedback platforms**, and **jury decisions**. Businesses use customer reviews and ratings to guide product development. Tech companies like Google and Netflix apply aggregated user behaviour to improve recommendations. It's also applied in **forecasting tools**, where a panel of diverse opinions is often more accurate than one forecaster.

Key Insights

- Crowds outperform experts when conditions include **diversity**, **independence**, and **aggregation**.

- Groupthink and conformity destroy the model's effectiveness.

- The model fails when the crowd is biased, uninformed, or lacks independence.

- Structured crowds (e.g., prediction markets) outperform informal ones.

Conclusion

The Wisdom of the Crowd teaches us that, under the right conditions, **many minds are better than one**. By leveraging group diversity and independence, we can tap into powerful collective intelligence—provided we know how to ask, listen, and aggregate well.

36. Relative Deprivation

Mental Model: Relative Deprivation – A Breakdown

Theory

Relative Deprivation is a psychological and sociological concept that refers to the feeling of dissatisfaction or resentment that arises when individuals or groups believe they are **worse off compared to others,** even if their own situation is objectively adequate. The focus is not on **absolute conditions,** but on **perceived inequality.** This mental model helps explain why people who have their basic needs met may still feel discontented when they see others doing better.

Developed in the mid-20th century and popularized by sociologist **Samuel Stouffer**, the theory suggests that social comparison, not actual deprivation, is often the catalyst for unrest, frustration, or ambition.

Example

Consider two employees at a company: both earn $60,000 a year. If one learns that a colleague in a similar role earns $70,000, despite similar performance, dissatisfaction may arise—even though nothing about their personal circumstances has changed. This is **relative deprivation** in action: the comparison creates a sense of unfairness, not the actual income level.

Why It Works

Relative deprivation works because humans are naturally **social comparators**. We constantly evaluate our standing by observing those around us. This mechanism helped early humans navigate status, cooperation, and competition, but in modern society, it often backfires— especially in the age of social media, where curated lifestyles amplify perceived inequality.

Emotions such as envy, resentment, and injustice stem from these comparisons and can influence behaviour far more than objective well-being.

How It Works

- An individual evaluates their condition relative to a reference group.

- If they perceive themselves as worse off, emotional discomfort follows.

- This discomfort can lead to changes in behaviour: disengagement, protest, or striving.

- Over time, widespread relative deprivation can influence group dynamics or social movements.

Application

Understanding this model is critical in **management, politics, marketing, education**, and **social justice advocacy**. Leaders must be aware that perceived inequality can damage morale more than absolute hardship. Marketers use this principle to trigger desire by showcasing lifestyles that create aspirational comparisons. Politicians often tap into relative deprivation to mobilize voters who feel "left behind," regardless of actual economic metrics.

Key Insights

- Satisfaction is heavily shaped by comparison, not just conditions.

- Fairness often matters more than absolute success.

- Managing expectations and transparency can reduce perceived deprivation.

- Social media intensifies this effect by distorting what's "normal."

Conclusion

Relative Deprivation reveals how human satisfaction and motivation are shaped by **perception, not reality**. By recognizing the power of comparison, we can build more empathetic systems, reduce unnecessary dissatisfaction, and make better decisions rooted in understanding—not illusion.

37. Social Loafing

Mental Model: Social Loafing – A Breakdown

Theory

Social Loafing is a psychological phenomenon where individuals **exert less effort** when working in a group than when working alone. The concept was first identified by **Max Ringelmann**, a French agricultural engineer, who noticed that people pulling a rope in a team applied less force per person than when pulling alone. The more people involved, the **less individual accountability**, and the lower the motivation to give full effort.

Social loafing is especially common in tasks where individual contributions are not easily measurable or where the group lacks strong cohesion, shared purpose, or clear structure. It's a critical concept in **organizational behaviour**, **team dynamics**, and **motivation theory**.

Example

Imagine a group of students assigned a group project. Initially enthusiastic, some group members contribute less over time, relying on others to carry the workload. The effort becomes uneven, and resentment may build among high-performing members. This is classic social loafing: some participants feel their contribution won't be noticed or necessary, so they disengage.

Why It Works

Social loafing works because of **diffusion of responsibility**. When many people share a task, individuals often believe someone else will step up. Without direct accountability or visibility, personal motivation declines. Additionally, when rewards or outcomes are equally shared, individuals may perceive it as more efficient to **conserve energy** while benefiting from the group's effort.

Psychologically, it also reduces the pressure to perform, as attention shifts from individual excellence to **blending into the group**.

How It Works

- A group is formed to complete a task.

- Individuals perceive reduced personal accountability.

- Effort diminishes, especially if roles are unclear or leadership is weak.

- Group performance suffers; high-effort members may feel exploited.

- The cycle can repeat unless structure and motivation are reinforced.

Application

This model is crucial in **team management, education, remote work, project planning**, and **performance evaluation**. To combat social loafing, leaders can assign **clear individual responsibilities**, provide **feedback**, and establish **shared goals**. In agile or high-performing teams, visibility and mutual respect reduce loafing. Remote teams, in particular, benefit from clarity and recognition systems to maintain engagement.

Key Insights

- People work harder when they feel **seen**, **needed**, and **accountable**.

- Group size and task visibility influence effort levels.

- Rewarding group success alone can demotivate top contributors.

- Effective teams balance **collaboration with individual ownership**.

Conclusion

The Social Loafing mental model reminds us that **shared responsibility can dilute effort**. By designing systems that recognize individual contributions within group contexts, we promote engagement, fairness, and collective success.

38. Status Seeking

Mental Model: Status Seeking – A Breakdown

Theory

Status Seeking is a psychological and sociological mental model that describes the human drive to improve or signal one's **social standing** within a group or society. Rooted in evolutionary biology and hierarchical social structures, status—whether earned or displayed—has long been associated with **access to resources, influence, and mating opportunities**. In modern life, status may be conveyed through wealth, titles, achievements, fashion, or online presence.

While the desire for status isn't inherently negative, it can influence behaviour in powerful, often subconscious ways—shaping consumption, career choices, affiliations, and even morality.

Example

Consider luxury branding. A person might buy an expensive watch not for its technical superiority, but because it signals wealth and refinement. The brand becomes a **status symbol**. Even if a cheaper alternative offers the same functionality, the expensive version provides social value. This illustrates status-seeking in consumer behaviour: the value lies not in the product, but in how it is **perceived by others**.

Why It Works

Status seeking works because social animals, including humans, are wired to care deeply about **relative position**. Status can provide tangible benefits (promotions, respect, resources) and intangible ones (esteem, admiration, influence). Psychologically, it satisfies needs for **belonging, identity, and recognition**.

From an evolutionary perspective, higher status often meant better chances of survival and reproduction. Today, these instincts still drive us, though the symbols of status have shifted from physical dominance to material, cultural, or digital signals.

How It Works

- Individuals observe social norms and cues about what is valued.

- They pursue behaviours, possessions, or achievements that signal alignment with those values.

- Social comparison reinforces the hierarchy: people assess themselves and others constantly.

- Success leads to validation, which fuels further status-seeking behaviours.

- Over time, entire markets, trends, or identities form around status signalling.

Application

Status seeking plays a central role in **marketing,**

leadership, workplace dynamics, education, and **social media**. Brands leverage it by turning products into badges of identity. Leaders can use it to motivate teams through recognition, not just rewards. In education, students may strive more for status (grades, honours) than intrinsic learning.

Key Insights

- People often act not for utility, but for appearance.

- Status is relative—raising yours often means lowering someone else's.

- Public visibility increases the intensity of status-driven behaviour.

- Status can motivate excellence or foster insecurity and rivalry.

Conclusion

The Status Seeking mental model helps explain much of human behaviour—especially in competitive, image-conscious environments. By understanding this drive, we can design better systems, incentives, and cultures that promote **healthy ambition over hollow signalling**.

39. Enclothed Cognition

Mental Model: Enclothed Cognition – A Breakdown

Theory

Enclothed Cognition is a psychological concept that refers to the **influence clothing has on the wearer's cognitive processes, behaviour, and performance**. The term was introduced by researchers Hajo Adam and Adam Galinsky in a 2012 study, where they explored how wearing specific types of clothing affects not just how we are perceived by others—but how we **perceive ourselves**.

The central idea is that clothes carry **symbolic meaning**, and when we wear them, we may psychologically adopt the associated traits. For example, wearing a lab coat not only changes how others see you—it can actually make you more focused, careful, or analytical, because the garment symbolizes intelligence and precision.

Example

In the original study, participants who wore a lab coat identified as a "doctor's coat" performed better on attention tasks than those wearing the same coat described as a "painter's coat" or those not wearing a coat at all. The difference was not just the physical garment, but the **meaning assigned to it** and how that meaning influenced cognition.

Why It Works

Enclothed cognition works because **clothing is deeply embedded with social and psychological associations**. When we put on clothes linked to a role or identity (e.g. a suit, uniform, or athletic wear), we subconsciously begin to **adopt the mindset** that fits the role. This psychological priming boosts self-awareness, confidence, or focus depending on the clothing's symbolism.

Our brains link clothing to **social scripts**—predefined expectations about how people in certain clothes behave. By dressing the part, we unconsciously begin acting the part.

How It Works

- A person wears a garment associated with a particular role or trait.

- That garment activates psychological associations (e.g. "this is what a leader wears").

- These associations subtly shift the wearer's behaviour, posture, self-talk, and focus.

- The effect is strongest when the garment is worn and its symbolism is consciously acknowledged.

Application

This model is applicable in **leadership, education, performance coaching, branding, and therapy**. Professionals can dress strategically to feel more authoritative or capable. Schools or teams can use uniforms to foster focus and unity. Therapists might use costume-based role play to help clients access new emotional states or self-concepts.

Key Insights

- Clothing doesn't just affect appearance—it influences identity and performance.

- Symbolism matters: belief in the meaning of clothing amplifies its effect.

- Dress intentionally for the role you want to embody.

- Self-perception can be shaped externally, not just internally.

Conclusion

The Enclothed Cognition mental model shows that **what we wear affects how we think and act**. By understanding this link, we can dress not just to impress—but to enhance cognition, confidence, and performance from the inside out.

40. Cultural Lag

Mental Model: Cultural Lag – A Breakdown

Theory

Cultural Lag is a sociological concept that explains the **delay between technological innovation and the cultural, legal, or ethical adaptations** required to cope with it. Coined by sociologist **William Fielding Ogburn** in the early 20th century, the idea highlights how **material culture** (technology, inventions, infrastructure) often evolves **faster** than **non-material culture** (laws, values, norms, institutions).

As a result, society often finds itself unprepared to fully integrate or regulate new technologies or practices, leading to ethical dilemmas, regulatory gaps, and social tension.

Example

A current example is **artificial intelligence (AI)**. While AI has rapidly advanced—powering everything from facial recognition to automated hiring—laws, educational systems, and social norms have lagged behind. Issues around privacy, surveillance, job displacement, and algorithmic bias have emerged faster than society can collectively agree on how to manage them. The **technology leads, but culture struggles to keep up**.

Why It Works

Cultural lag works because **human systems are slower to change** than technological systems. Creating a new tool can take months, but shifting societal values or drafting legislation takes years—sometimes decades. This mismatch creates a **transitional period** where people interact with new realities using outdated frameworks.

Psychologically, humans also resist change due to habit, tradition, or fear of the unknown. Institutions—governments, schools, legal systems—are designed to be stable, not reactive. Thus, when innovation accelerates, lag is almost inevitable.

How It Works

- A technological innovation is introduced and rapidly adopted.

- Society lacks updated norms, laws, or understanding to integrate it responsibly.

- Friction occurs—often seen in confusion, resistance, or controversy.

- Over time, culture "catches up" through public discourse, regulation, and education.

Application

This model is crucial in **policy-making, ethics, education, business strategy**, and **social advocacy**. Lawmakers can anticipate and reduce lag by creating adaptable legal frameworks. Educators can revise curricula to prepare students for emerging realities. Businesses that acknowledge cultural lag can innovate responsibly and win public trust. Social activists use this model to highlight gaps and push for change.

Key Insights

- Technological change outpaces cultural adaptation.

- Lag creates a window of confusion, risk, or resistance.

- Anticipating lag helps societies and organizations adapt more wisely.

- Addressing lag requires collaboration between technologists, ethicists, and lawmakers.

Conclusion

Cultural Lag reveals that **progress is not always evenly distributed**—especially between what we build and how we behave. By understanding and planning for the lag, we can close the gap between innovation and ethics, ensuring change is both forward-thinking and human-centred.

Mathematical and Logical Models:

41. Law of Large Numbers

Mental Model: Law of Large Numbers – A Breakdown

Theory

The **Law of Large Numbers (LLN)** is a fundamental principle in probability and statistics stating that as the **number of trials increases**, the **average of the results will converge toward the expected value**. In simple terms, the more times an event is repeated, the closer the observed outcomes will reflect the true underlying probability.

Formally developed by **Jacob Bernoulli** in the 18th century, this law underpins much of statistical inference and data analysis. While individual outcomes may vary wildly, large sample sizes tend to smooth out randomness, revealing consistent patterns.

Example

Imagine flipping a fair coin. In 10 flips, you might get 7 heads and 3 tails—suggesting a skewed result. But after 10,000 flips, you'll likely get very close to 50% heads and 50% tails. This is the Law of Large Numbers in action: **short-term results are noisy, but long-term results are stable**.

Why It Works

The LLN works because random fluctuations balance out over time. While any single outcome is subject to chance, repeated trials reduce the effect of anomalies. The larger the sample, the more **statistically reliable** the average becomes. This principle is essential in understanding **risk, probability, and long-term forecasting**.

It also corrects for **misleading intuition**. Humans often overreact to small sample sizes, mistaking short-term variation for meaningful patterns.

How It Works

- A random process is repeated many times (e.g., rolling dice, polling voters).

- Each individual trial has variability, but collectively the data trends toward the expected mean.

- The more trials conducted, the smaller the **margin of error**.

- This principle assumes trials are independent and conditions are stable.

Application
LLN is vital in **finance, insurance, medicine, polling, gambling, quality control**, and **scientific research**. Actuaries use it to price insurance based on large population data. Investors rely on it to judge long-term market returns, despite short-term volatility. In science, it validates that experiments with sufficient sample sizes yield reliable conclusions.

Understanding LLN helps distinguish between **luck and skill**, and why **short-term performance** is not always predictive of long-term outcomes.

Key Insights

- Small samples often mislead; large samples reveal truth.

- Consistency emerges through scale, not isolated outcomes.

- It's essential to wait for enough data before drawing conclusions.

- LLN supports rational, long-term thinking in uncertain domains.

Conclusion

The Law of Large Numbers reminds us that **repetition reveals reality**. In a world full of randomness, this model teaches patience, scepticism toward small samples, and confidence in the power of well-collected data over time.

42. Small Wins

Mental Model: Small Wins – A Breakdown

Theory

The **Small Wins** mental model suggests that large, complex problems are best approached through a series of **incremental, manageable actions** that build momentum over time. Rather than aiming for sweeping transformation, progress is achieved through a **chain of minor successes**. This concept is rooted in the work of organizational theorist **Karl Weick**, who proposed that small, concrete achievements can reduce psychological barriers and make large challenges seem more approachable.

Small wins work by reframing problems: instead of feeling overwhelmed by the full scope of a goal, individuals and teams focus on what can be accomplished today—then use that momentum to take the next step.

Example

Consider someone trying to lose 50 pounds. That goal might feel daunting and unachievable. However, if they break it into small wins—like walking 10 minutes a day, replacing soda with water, or preparing a healthy lunch— they create **manageable steps** that build confidence and consistency. Each small success makes the next one feel more attainable, fuelling progress.

Why It Works

Small wins work because they **build self-efficacy** (the belief in one's ability to succeed) and **reduce inertia**. Large problems often create emotional resistance—stress, anxiety, or avoidance. But achieving a small, specific goal triggers a **positive feedback loop**: progress boosts motivation, which in turn encourages further action. Additionally, small wins reduce risk and increase learning opportunities without overwhelming cognitive resources.

How It Works

- A large challenge is broken down into smaller, achievable goals.

- Each small goal is pursued with focus and clarity.

- Success provides emotional and psychological rewards.

- Confidence, skill, and momentum accumulate with each win.

- Over time, small wins compound into significant progress.

Application

This model is widely applicable in **habit formation, leadership, therapy, education, project management**, and **organizational change**. Coaches and therapists use it to guide behaviour change. Leaders implement it to navigate complex change in teams. Product teams use agile development to iterate through small, testable versions. It also plays a key role in systems design, where complex improvements often emerge through small, adaptive steps.

Key Insights

- Big results come from compounding small efforts.

- Progress is more sustainable when it feels achievable.

- Small wins build psychological momentum and reduce fear.

- Framing challenges as sequences of wins creates clarity and action.

Conclusion

The Small Wins mental model teaches that **meaningful change doesn't require dramatic action—it requires consistency**. By focusing on modest, continuous progress, we turn intention into habit and complexity into clarity, unlocking long-term success one small step at a time.

43. Power of Weak Ties

Mental Model: Power of Weak Ties – A Breakdown

Theory

The **Power of Weak Ties** is a sociological concept introduced by **Mark Granovetter** in his influential 1973 paper, *The Strength of Weak Ties*. The theory challenges the assumption that our closest relationships (strong ties) are the most valuable. Instead, Granovetter showed that **weak ties—acquaintances, distant colleagues, casual contacts—often provide greater access to new opportunities, ideas, and information** than our inner circle.

Strong ties tend to exist within tight-knit, overlapping networks where everyone knows each other and shares similar information. Weak ties, however, connect us to **different social circles**, making them essential bridges to novel resources and perspectives.

Example

Imagine you're looking for a new job. Your close friends may already be aware of the same opportunities as you. But a distant former coworker, who moves in a different professional network, might inform you about a role you'd never have discovered otherwise. Studies consistently show that many people find jobs through **weak ties**, not their closest connections.

Why It Works

This model works because **information diversity** is greater in wider, looser networks. Strong ties offer depth and emotional support, but they often lack **novelty**. Weak ties expose us to **new environments, people, and perspectives** that don't exist in our immediate social circles.

Additionally, people are often more willing to help weak ties because it comes with **lower relational expectations**, creating a cleaner exchange of value.

How It Works

- Individuals maintain both strong (close) and weak (distant) relationships.

- Weak ties serve as **bridges** between otherwise disconnected groups.

- These bridges provide **access to information** and opportunities not available in the individual's core network.

- By activating weak ties (reaching out, reconnecting), individuals can unlock new pathways.

Application

This model is crucial in **networking, career development, innovation, recruitment**, and **idea generation**.

Entrepreneurs use weak ties to validate ideas. Researchers collaborate across fields through weak ties to spark interdisciplinary innovation. Professionals can cultivate broader influence by investing in diverse, low-maintenance relationships over time. Social platforms like LinkedIn are built around this principle.

Key Insights

- Your strongest opportunities often lie just outside your immediate circle.

- Diversity in connections creates resilience and innovation.

- Maintaining weak ties doesn't require constant effort—just periodic engagement.

- Weak ties are efficient: high return with low investment.

Conclusion

The Power of Weak Ties teaches us that **breadth often beats depth** in certain contexts. By nurturing diverse, low-friction connections across social and professional boundaries, we unlock access to new ideas, opportunities, and perspectives we wouldn't otherwise reach.

44. Logarithmic Growth

Mental Model: Logarithmic Growth – A Breakdown

Theory

Logarithmic growth is a mathematical model in which growth happens **rapidly at first**, but then **slows down over time**, approaching a ceiling or limit. Unlike linear growth (steady rate) or exponential growth (increasing rate), logarithmic growth shows **diminishing returns** as input increases. It is often represented by a curve that rises steeply at the beginning and then flattens out.

This model is common in **learning curves, fitness progress, technological adoption**, and **performance improvement**, where the biggest gains occur early, followed by progressively smaller improvements despite continued effort.

Example

Consider someone learning a new language. In the first few weeks, they pick up basic phrases, vocabulary, and grammar rapidly. Progress feels fast and rewarding. But as they advance, new words and rules become subtler, and improvement requires significantly more effort for smaller gains. Their growth follows a logarithmic curve—**steep early, then gradual**.

Why It Works

Logarithmic growth reflects the **low-hanging fruit**

principle: initial efforts yield large returns because there's so much to gain. But as you get closer to mastery or saturation, progress becomes more difficult. Psychologically, this creates a **motivation challenge**, as the perceived value of effort diminishes over time.

This model helps us set more **realistic expectations**, especially in skill development or long-term projects. It explains why early progress feels easy and satisfying, while later stages demand discipline, strategy, and patience.

How It Works

- A system begins with low input or effort.

- Early gains are substantial because there's little resistance or complexity.

- As input continues, gains start to diminish due to natural limits or complexity barriers.

- Progress slows but continues incrementally toward an upper bound.

Application
Logarithmic growth is essential in **education, health, business, personal development**, and **technology**. Educators use it to explain why students may plateau after initial improvements. Product designers see it in user engagement curves. In fitness or business growth, recognizing this model helps avoid burnout by adjusting expectations over time.

Understanding this curve also supports better **resource allocation**—pushing hard at the start can maximize returns, but diminishing gains later suggest it's smarter to pivot or diversify effort.

Key Insights

- Big gains often come early; mastery takes exponentially more work.

- Don't expect constant returns from constant effort.

- Plateaus are normal and not a sign of failure.

- Smart strategy involves shifting goals as returns diminish.

Conclusion

The Logarithmic Growth mental model reminds us that **initial progress is not always predictive of long-term results**. By embracing the curve—fast start, slow climb—we develop patience, refine our tactics, and sustain growth without being discouraged by diminishing returns.

45. Exponential Decay

Mental Model: Exponential Decay – A Breakdown

Theory

Exponential decay is a mathematical model that describes processes where a quantity **decreases at a rate proportional to its current value**. In simpler terms, the **larger the quantity, the faster it shrinks**—and as it gets smaller, the rate of decrease slows down. This creates a steep drop early on, followed by a gradual tapering off.

Exponential decay is the mirror image of exponential growth. Instead of compounding gains, it reflects **compounding losses** or **diminishing quantities** over time. This model is widely used in **physics, biology, economics,** and **information science**, often describing things like radioactive decay, memory retention, or depreciation of assets.

Example

A classic example is **memory loss**. When we learn something new, we remember most of it right away. But within hours or days, a large portion is forgotten unless reinforced. According to **Ebbinghaus's Forgetting Curve**, memory retention drops sharply after learning, then decays more slowly over time. The rate of forgetting is exponential—**fast initially, then slower**.

Why It Works

Exponential decay works because systems lose energy, information, or value in ways that **compound** over time. Whether it's attention, battery power, or asset value, each moment subtracts a percentage of what's left—not a fixed amount. This makes the process **predictable but non-linear**, helping us model systems that naturally decline unless maintained.

Psychologically, this model also explains **why immediate action** is so crucial—because the early stages of decay are where the most loss occurs.

How It Works

- A process begins with a starting value.

- At each interval, a fixed **percentage** of that value is lost.

- The loss compounds: large at first, smaller over time.

- Eventually, the value asymptotically approaches zero but never quite reaches it.

Application

This model is essential in **project management (interest decay), learning retention, marketing (attention span), finance (asset depreciation), and health (drug elimination).** For example, understanding exponential decay helps educators design effective review cycles to combat rapid forgetting. Businesses apply it in customer engagement strategies to reconnect before interest fades too much.

Key Insights

- Systems degrade faster than we expect—especially early on.

- Without reinforcement or renewal, value erodes quickly.

- Early intervention can drastically slow decay.

- Not all decline is linear; some systems fall off quickly then plateau.

Conclusion

The Exponential Decay mental model teaches that **time erodes value rapidly unless maintained**. Recognizing and planning for early-stage decline—whether in memory, attention, or resources—helps us act faster, preserve effectiveness, and sustain what matters over time.

46. Inverse Relationship

Mental Model: Inverse Relationship – A Breakdown

Theory

An **Inverse Relationship** (also known as an inverse correlation or negative relationship) describes a situation where **one variable increases as another decreases**. Mathematically, this is often represented as $y=kx$ $y = \frac{k}{x}$, where k k is a constant. In practical terms, it means the variables move in **opposite directions**.

Inverse relationships are common in economics, physics, biology, and behavioural science. They help explain trade-offs, scarcity, and diminishing returns. Unlike a direct relationship—where more input yields more output—in an inverse relationship, **more of one thing leads to less of another**.

Example

A classic example is the **relationship between price and demand** in economics. As the **price of a product increases**, demand generally **decreases**, and vice versa (assuming all else is equal). This is the basis of the **law of demand**. Consumers buy less when prices rise, illustrating an inverse relationship between the two variables.

Why It Works

Inverse relationships work because **resources and preferences are limited**, and systems often operate under constraints. When one variable stretches or consumes more of a resource, another must give. In social or natural systems, trade-offs and balancing forces are ever-present. Recognizing inverse dynamics helps avoid over-optimizing one metric at the cost of another.

Psychologically, this model counters simplistic "more is better" thinking by emphasizing **balance** and **cost-benefit dynamics**.

How It Works

- Two variables are functionally or behaviourally connected.

- As one increases, it places pressure or limitations on the other.

- The system responds by reducing or weakening the second variable.

- The relationship can be nonlinear or context-specific but maintains the opposite directional trend.

Application
The inverse relationship model is vital in **resource allocation, time management, economics, physiology**, and **risk assessment**. In fitness, for example, **rest and intensity** are inversely related: more intense workouts require longer recovery. In business, **risk and return** often exhibit an inverse balance—lower risk generally yields lower returns.

In decision-making, this model helps clarify **trade-offs**: speed vs. quality, cost vs. convenience, depth vs. breadth. It encourages a more nuanced, systems-level view.

Key Insights

- More of one thing usually means less of another.

- Maximizing one metric can degrade another if not balanced.

- Trade-offs are not failures; they are structural realities.

- Inverse thinking helps manage expectations and avoid tunnel vision.

Conclusion

The Inverse Relationship mental model reminds us that **gains often come with costs**. By recognizing when variables are oppositely linked, we can make smarter, more balanced choices—strategically adjusting one without unintentionally compromising another.

47. Decision Trees

Mental Model: Decision Trees – A Breakdown

Theory

A **Decision Tree** is a mental and analytical model used to **map out decisions and their possible outcomes** in a structured, branching format. Each node in the tree represents a choice or a chance event, and each branch represents the possible consequences of those decisions. Decision trees help individuals and organizations **evaluate options, estimate risks, and weigh potential rewards** in complex or uncertain situations.

This model is rooted in **probability theory, logic, and decision analysis**, and is commonly used in fields like **business strategy, machine learning, finance**, and **medicine**. It turns abstract decision-making into a **visual, step-by-step process**.

Example

Imagine a company deciding whether to launch a new product. They can either launch it now or delay it to gather more customer feedback. A decision tree would show the two choices as branches, with further branches exploring different outcomes: if they launch now, will customers respond well or poorly? If they delay, will the extra research improve success or waste time? Each outcome is assigned a **probability and value**, allowing for clearer comparison.

Why It Works

Decision trees work because they **decompose complex decisions into manageable parts**. They force explicit consideration of possible actions and their consequences, helping avoid emotional, reactive, or biased decision-making. By quantifying outcomes and mapping pathways, decision trees provide clarity, especially under uncertainty.

They also encourage **probabilistic thinking**—helping users recognize that not all decisions guarantee success, but can be optimized for expected value.

How It Works

- Define the decision point (root).

- List possible choices (branches).

- For each choice, outline possible outcomes or future decisions.

- Assign probabilities and potential payoffs or costs to each branch.

- Evaluate and compare branches to determine the most favourable path.

Application

Decision trees are widely used in **strategic planning, data science, legal reasoning, medical diagnosis**, and **personal decision-making**. In business, they help guide investment or marketing choices. In machine learning, decision tree algorithms classify data based on branching questions. In personal life, decision trees can clarify career moves, financial plans, or risk scenarios.

Key Insights

- Complex decisions are more manageable when broken into parts.

- Visualizing consequences improves clarity and foresight.

- Good decisions focus on **expected value**, not just outcomes.

- Decision trees promote objectivity by surfacing assumptions and probabilities.

Conclusion

The Decision Tree mental model teaches us to **think in branches, not binaries**. By laying out choices and consequences systematically, we make smarter, more strategic decisions—even in the face of uncertainty.

48. Monte Carlo Simulation

Mental Model: Monte Carlo Simulation – A Breakdown

Theory

Monte Carlo Simulation is a decision-making and forecasting model that uses **random sampling and statistical modelling** to estimate the probability of different outcomes in complex systems. Named after the Monte Carlo casino due to its reliance on chance, this model allows individuals and organizations to **understand variability, risk, and uncertainty** in a structured, repeatable way.

Instead of relying on fixed-point predictions or average-case assumptions, Monte Carlo methods generate **thousands (or millions) of simulations** based on input variables, producing a distribution of possible results. It's commonly used in **finance, engineering, project management, data science**, and **climate modelling**.

Example

Consider an investor assessing the potential return of a new portfolio. Instead of assuming a single rate of return (say 6% annually), a Monte Carlo simulation models **a range of returns**, incorporating historical volatility, inflation, and market fluctuations. By running 10,000 simulated investment paths, the investor sees that 80% of outcomes fall between 4% and 8%, giving a **probabilistic understanding** of the risk/reward profile.

Why It Works

Monte Carlo simulations work because real-world systems are rarely linear or certain. Many variables interact in unpredictable ways. This method embraces **randomness** to reveal the range of possibilities, helping avoid **overconfidence in single-point forecasts**. By simulating thousands of scenarios, decision-makers get a richer view of risk, including **best-case, worst-case, and most-likely outcomes**.

How It Works

- Define the problem and identify key input variables.

- Assign a **probability distribution** to each uncertain input (e.g., cost, demand, return).

- Use a computer to **randomly sample** from those distributions.

- Calculate the result based on the sampled inputs.

- Repeat the process thousands of times to generate a distribution of outcomes.

- Analyse the output to assess risk, likelihood, and sensitivity.

Application

Monte Carlo simulations are used in **financial planning**

(e.g., retirement models), **engineering** (safety risk analysis), **drug testing, supply chain management**, and **policy analysis**. Project managers use it to estimate completion timelines with uncertainty. Scientists apply it to model weather systems or disease spread under different assumptions.

Key Insights

- Uncertainty is not something to ignore—it can be modelled.

- Single-point estimates are often misleading.

- Probabilistic thinking improves real-world planning.

- Simulations reveal not just "what could happen," but **how often**.

Conclusion

The Monte Carlo Simulation model teaches us to **embrace uncertainty by quantifying it**. Rather than guessing or hoping, it offers a structured, data-driven way to explore outcomes, test assumptions, and make better-informed decisions under conditions of complexity and risk.

49. Bell Curve (Normal Distribution)

Mental Model: Bell Curve (Normal Distribution) – A Breakdown

Theory

The **Bell Curve**, also known as the **Normal Distribution**, is a statistical model describing how values are distributed in many naturally occurring systems. It's called a "bell curve" due to its distinctive shape: most data clusters around a central average (mean), and frequencies taper off symmetrically on either side. This curve is foundational in probability theory and statistics.

In a perfect normal distribution:

- The **mean, median, and mode are equal**.

- About **68%** of the data lies within one standard deviation from the mean.

- Around **95%** falls within two standard deviations.

- Roughly **99.7%** lies within three standard deviations.

This model is critical because it reflects the behaviour of many real-world phenomena—such as heights, test scores, measurement errors, and human traits—under stable and random conditions.

Example

A common example is **IQ scores**. IQ is designed to follow a normal distribution with a mean of 100 and a standard deviation of 15. That means:

- Most people (68%) score between 85 and 115.

- Very high or very low scores (outside 130 or below 70) are statistically rare.

This structure allows psychologists, educators, and policymakers to make meaningful comparisons and identify outliers.

Why It Works

The Bell Curve works because of the **Central Limit Theorem**, which states that the average of many independent, random variables tends to follow a normal distribution—even if the original variables themselves do not. It also reflects how variation in nature often centres around a norm, with extreme values being less common due to systemic constraints or natural balancing forces.

How It Works

- A dataset is collected and plotted based on frequency.

- If the data follows a normal distribution, it will show a symmetrical, bell-shaped curve.

- Standard deviations are used to understand the spread and likelihood of values.

- Predictions, comparisons, or decisions are made based on how far a value is from the mean.

Application

The Bell Curve is used in **education (grading), finance (risk modelling), quality control, psychology, healthcare**, and **hiring**. It helps identify norms, assess probabilities, detect anomalies, and design interventions. For example, in manufacturing, a product's consistency can be monitored by checking how far variations deviate from the average.

Key Insights

- Most occurrences in nature follow a central trend with rare extremes.

- Standard deviations help quantify how "unusual" a result is.

- Assumptions of normality help simplify complex data—but not all systems follow it.

- Overreliance on normality can miss fat tails or skewed distributions.

Conclusion

The Bell Curve mental model provides a powerful lens for understanding **variation, probability, and predictability**. By appreciating its shape and limitations, we can make more informed decisions in fields that depend on data, measurement, and human behaviour.

50. Symmetry Breaking

Mental Model: Symmetry Breaking – A Breakdown

Theory

Symmetry Breaking is a concept from physics and systems theory that explains how systems that start off in a balanced or symmetrical state can **suddenly shift into an asymmetrical one**, creating differentiation, structure, or direction. While originally used to describe particle physics and cosmology (such as the formation of matter after the Big Bang), it is a broadly applicable mental model for understanding **how order and complexity emerge from uniformity**.

Symmetry breaking occurs when small fluctuations or external pressures disrupt a balanced state, causing the system to "choose" one configuration over another. Once this balance is disturbed, the symmetry cannot be restored without significant intervention, and the system evolves in a new direction.

Example

A classic non-physics example is **handedness** in humans. While the human body is largely symmetrical, most people are either right- or left-handed. There's no inherent reason for one side to dominate at birth, but small genetic or environmental factors create **asymmetry**, leading to consistent preference and structure.

In business, consider a startup environment where many ideas appear equally viable. A seemingly minor advantage—like one founder's prior experience or a random early success—can "break the symmetry" and push resources and attention toward one path, shaping the entire trajectory of the company.

Why It Works
Symmetry breaking works because **real systems are sensitive to initial conditions**. Though two options may start as equally viable, slight differences can be amplified over time, leading to **path dependence**. The symmetry isn't stable—external nudges, randomness, or internal dynamics inevitably shift balance, pushing the system toward a dominant state.

How It Works

- A system starts in a symmetrical, balanced configuration.

- A small fluctuation (random, structural, or intentional) tips the balance.

- That disturbance is amplified, reinforcing the new asymmetrical state.

- The system evolves in a specific direction based on that early deviation.

Application
Symmetry breaking is useful in **evolutionary biology, entrepreneurship, game theory, creative strategy, and**

change management. In leadership, recognizing that small actions or symbolic choices can tip a group in one direction is powerful. In markets, a tiny competitive edge can establish dominance over time. In biology, random mutations break symmetry, enabling diversity and adaptation.

Key Insights

- Small initial conditions can lead to big, irreversible outcomes.

- Symmetry often hides potential instability or tipping points.

- Early choices matter more than we think—they shape the system's evolution.

- Once symmetry breaks, systems often "lock in" to new behaviours.

Conclusion

The Symmetry Breaking mental model reminds us that **order emerges from imbalance**. Understanding how tiny, early differences shape complex outcomes helps us make better strategic decisions in systems where stakes are high and starting conditions matter.

Leadership and Management Models:

51. Span of Control

Mental Model: Span of Control – A Breakdown

Theory

Span of Control is a key principle in organizational design and management that refers to the **number of direct reports a manager or leader can effectively supervise**. First introduced by management theorist **Lyndall Urwick**, the concept helps determine how hierarchical or flat an organization should be. A **narrow span** means fewer subordinates per manager, resulting in more layers of hierarchy. A **wide span** means more subordinates per manager and a flatter structure.

The ideal span of control depends on factors like task complexity, managerial competence, technology support, and team autonomy. Balancing the span of control is crucial to ensure **efficiency, communication, accountability**, and **employee development**.

Example

In a customer support department, a team leader might effectively oversee 10 support agents handling routine, scripted inquiries. However, in a product development team where tasks are creative and interdependent, a manager may only be able to supervise 4 or 5 engineers effectively. The more complex and variable the work, the narrower the optimal span.

Why It Works

This model works because **cognitive bandwidth, communication channels, and leadership quality are limited resources**. A manager with too many direct reports may become a bottleneck, miss performance issues, or fail to develop their team. Conversely, too narrow a span can create **bureaucracy**, slow decision-making, and inflate management costs without added value.

Span of control affects **responsiveness, morale**, and **clarity of responsibility**. It also shapes how organizations scale and how well they adapt to change.

How It Works

- Assess the complexity, variability, and interdependence of team tasks.

- Match managerial capacity with the number of direct reports.

- Adjust for supporting systems like communication tools or delegation structures.

- Re-evaluate span regularly as teams grow or functions evolve.

Application

Span of control is critical in **organizational design, leadership development, operations**, and **start-up scaling**. Startups often begin with wide spans for speed but narrow them as roles specialize. In healthcare or aviation, where safety and complexity are high, spans are intentionally narrow. In contrast, standardized environments like call centres can afford wider spans.

Key Insights

- There is no "one-size-fits-all" span—it must fit context.

- Wider spans work when roles are clear, repetitive, and require little coordination.

- Narrow spans support coaching, quality control, and innovation.

- Technology can expand effective span through better communication and automation.

Conclusion

The Span of Control model teaches us that **effective leadership is not just about authority, but about capacity**. Managing the right number of people in the right way leads to better performance, healthier organizations, and more sustainable growth.

52. Pygmalion Effect

The **Pygmalion Effect**, also known as the **Rosenthal Effect**, is a psychological phenomenon where higher expectations lead to improved performance. It stems from the idea that people's performance aligns with the expectations placed upon them—if you believe someone will succeed, your behaviour unconsciously encourages their success.

Theoretical Basis

The theory was popularized by a 1968 study by psychologist Robert Rosenthal and school principal Lenore Jacobson. They told teachers that certain randomly selected students were expected to be "intellectual bloomers." By the end of the year, those students had significantly higher academic gains—despite no actual difference in ability. The conclusion: teacher expectations influenced student performance.

The Pygmalion Effect aligns with the self-fulfilling prophecy: if someone is expected to succeed, the resulting positive reinforcement and attention lead them to meet those expectations.

Example

Imagine a manager leading two new hires. She's told (falsely) that one has a top-tier background, while the other is average. Unconsciously, she offers more support, encouragement, and challenging tasks to the "top-tier" employee. That employee, feeling trusted and motivated, performs exceptionally. The other, sensing less belief in them, underperforms. The manager's belief shaped the outcome.

Why It Works

The Pygmalion Effect works because expectations influence behaviour, which then shapes outcomes. When leaders expect high performance, they often provide more attention, constructive feedback, and opportunities— boosting confidence and motivation. This feedback loop reinforces positive behaviour and improved results.

How It Works

It operates through **nonverbal cues**, **tone**, **opportunity allocation**, and **feedback quality**. A leader who expects success might offer more eye contact, positive reinforcement, and challenges that stretch an individual. These subtle signals foster a belief in the individual's ability, boosting self-efficacy. As individuals internalize that belief, they perform better.

Conversely, the **Golem Effect** (the negative counterpart) occurs when low expectations lead to poorer performance.

Application

The Pygmalion Effect has practical use in **education**, **workplace leadership**, **coaching**, and **parenting**. Teachers, managers, and mentors can foster growth by consciously maintaining and communicating high expectations.

Progressive organizations train leaders to be aware of unconscious bias and the impact of their expectations on team performance.

Key Insights

- Expectations act as self-fulfilling prophecies.

- Belief in others can be a powerful performance driver.

- Subtle cues and feedback impact self-perception and motivation.

- Leaders must be mindful of their assumptions and biases.

- Intentionally cultivating high expectations can elevate entire teams.

Ultimately, the Pygmalion Effect reveals the quiet but powerful role belief plays in shaping human potential.

53. Theory X and Theory Y

Theory X and Theory Y are management theories developed by Douglas McGregor in his 1960 book *"The Human Side of Enterprise."* These theories describe two contrasting views of workforce motivation and behaviour, and they underpin many modern approaches to leadership and organizational management.

Theoretical Basis

Theory X assumes employees are inherently lazy, dislike work, lack ambition, and must be coerced, controlled, or threatened with punishment to perform. This aligns with a top-down, authoritarian management style.

Theory Y, by contrast, posits that people are naturally motivated to work, seek responsibility, and can exercise self-direction and creativity if they are committed to objectives. It aligns with a participative management style that trusts and empowers employees.

These models aren't about what is true universally, but rather about how managers' assumptions about human nature influence their behaviour toward subordinates— and in turn, employee performance.

Example

Consider two managers:
Manager X closely monitors his team, sets strict rules, and

punishes mistakes. His employees disengage, do the bare minimum, and rarely offer new ideas.

Manager Y encourages autonomy, involves the team in decision-making, and supports development. Her team feels valued, contributes actively, and frequently innovates.

Why It Works

Theory Y works because it taps into intrinsic motivation—the internal desire to grow, achieve, and contribute. When employees feel trusted and involved, they reciprocate with higher engagement and performance. Conversely, Theory X can create a self-fulfilling prophecy: when people are treated as untrustworthy, they often conform to that expectation.

How It Works

Theory Y practices foster **psychological safety** and **job enrichment**. Managers set meaningful goals, provide feedback, and involve employees in decision-making. This aligns personal goals with organizational objectives, increasing commitment and satisfaction. In contrast, Theory X operates through strict oversight, rules, and extrinsic rewards or punishments.

Application

Theory Y is widely applied in **modern workplaces**, especially in knowledge industries, startups, and agile organizations. Companies like Google and Netflix promote autonomy and responsibility, aligning with Theory Y.

Theory X may still be used in repetitive or high-risk industries where tight control is necessary, like manufacturing or military operations.

Key Insights

- Managers' assumptions influence their leadership style, which in turn affects employee behaviour.

- Empowering people (Theory Y) often leads to innovation, loyalty, and performance.

- Over-controlling (Theory X) can breed resentment, disengagement, and compliance instead of commitment.

- The best managers may balance both theories depending on context and individual team members.

Ultimately, McGregor's model encourages managers to reflect on their beliefs about human motivation and adapt their style accordingly for better organizational outcomes.

54. Parkinson's Law of Triviality

Parkinson's Law of Triviality, also known as **bike shedding**, is a mental model coined by British naval historian and author C. Northcote Parkinson in 1957. It suggests that people often give disproportionate weight to trivial issues while neglecting more complex, significant matters. The term comes from Parkinson's observation that a committee would spend more time discussing the design of a bike shed (a relatively simple issue) than the construction of a nuclear power plant (a highly complex one).

Theoretical Basis

This law is rooted in human psychology. Most people feel more confident discussing familiar, easy-to-grasp topics than tackling complex or unfamiliar problems. In group settings, this often leads to extensive debate over minor issues while critical decisions are glossed over or delayed. The model reflects cognitive bias: people gravitate toward what they understand and can control, even when it's relatively unimportant.

Example

Imagine a corporate meeting to approve a $10 million project. The discussion on the core technical infrastructure (which is complex and requires specialized knowledge) is quickly passed over. But when it comes to choosing the colour for the new office furniture or the team's coffee machine, everyone has an opinion, and the discussion drags on for hours. The trivial issue consumes more time than the significant one.

Why It Works

It works—though dysfunctionally—because engaging with simple issues provides a sense of productivity and contribution. Discussing a complex subject like nuclear engineering can feel intimidating or exclusive. On the other hand, everyone can relate to the design of a bike shed or the taste of coffee, so they feel more comfortable offering opinions.

How It Works

The law operates through **cognitive ease** and **group dynamics**. In meetings or teams, members instinctively steer toward topics where they feel knowledgeable or safe. This results in excessive focus on low-impact issues and neglect of high-impact but intellectually demanding ones. It is often unintentional but leads to inefficient decision-making.

Application

Understanding Parkinson's Law of Triviality is valuable for **leaders**, **project managers**, and **decision-makers**. Awareness helps redirect energy toward high-leverage activities. In practice, this means structuring meetings around clear priorities, setting time limits for minor topics, and assigning experts to guide discussions on complex issues.

Key Insights

- People over-engage with topics they understand, even if they're unimportant.

- Trivial issues can consume more time than critical decisions.

- Leaders must guide focus toward what truly matters.

- Establishing structured agendas can reduce bike shedding.

- Decision-making quality improves when complexity is faced directly, not avoided.

By recognizing this mental trap, individuals and teams can resist the urge to over-focus on the trivial and make better use of their time and energy.

55. Lean Thinking

Lean Thinking is a mental model and management philosophy focused on maximizing value while minimizing waste. Originating from the Toyota Production System (TPS) and later popularized by James Womack and Daniel Jones in their book *"Lean Thinking"* (1996), it offers a systematic approach to improving efficiency, quality, and responsiveness in organizations.

Theoretical Basis

At its core, Lean Thinking is based on five principles:

1. **Value** – Define what truly matters to the customer.

2. **Value Stream** – Map all steps in the process and identify non-value-adding activities.

3. **Flow** – Ensure that value-creating steps occur in a tight sequence without delays.

4. **Pull** – Produce only what is needed, when it is needed.

5. **Perfection** – Continuously strive to improve processes and eliminate waste.

It views waste (muda) as anything that does not add value, including overproduction, waiting, unnecessary movement, excess inventory, defects, overprocessing, and underutilized talent.

Example

A software company adopts Lean Thinking in its development process. Instead of building full-scale products over months, it delivers small, valuable features weekly based on customer feedback. By mapping their workflow, they realize excessive time is spent on handovers between teams. They eliminate bottlenecks, integrate teams, and continuously test and improve. The result: faster delivery, higher quality, and better customer satisfaction.

Why It Works

Lean Thinking works because it aligns all activities with customer value and continuously improves based on feedback. By removing waste, organizations become more agile, cost-effective, and responsive. It also empowers employees to take ownership of improvements, leading to higher engagement and innovation.

How It Works

Lean Thinking operates through **visual management, feedback loops**, and **incremental improvements**. Tools like **value stream mapping, Kaizen (continuous improvement),** and **Just-in-Time production** help identify inefficiencies. Employees are trained to think critically about their work and contribute to systemic change rather than just doing tasks.

The mindset is proactive and iterative: instead of fixing problems only when they break, Lean seeks to prevent issues by improving the system continuously.

Application

Lean Thinking is widely applied in **manufacturing, software development (e.g., Lean Agile), healthcare, education**, and **service industries**. For example, hospitals use Lean to streamline patient care and reduce wait times, while startups use it to build products based on real user needs.

Key Insights

- Focus on value from the customer's perspective.

- Waste is often hidden in processes and must be actively identified.

- Small, continuous improvements compound into significant gains.

- Engaged teams and clear workflows are essential.

- Lean is a mindset, not just a toolkit—it thrives on culture change.

Lean Thinking enables organizations to do more with less—more value, less waste, and greater responsiveness in a fast-changing world.

56. T-shaped People

T-shaped People is a mental model used to describe individuals who possess deep expertise in one area (the vertical bar of the "T") and broad skills and knowledge across multiple disciplines (the horizontal bar). This concept originated in the 1990s, popularized by **David Guest** and embraced by organizations like **IDEO** and **McKinsey** to build innovative, collaborative teams.

Theoretical Basis

The vertical bar represents **depth**—a person's deep knowledge or specialization in a specific field (e.g., software engineering, graphic design, or data analysis). The horizontal bar represents **breadth**—a person's ability to collaborate across disciplines, understand other perspectives, and apply general knowledge across contexts.

T-shaped thinking contrasts with I-shaped individuals (deep but narrow expertise) and underscores the need for adaptability and teamwork in complex, modern work environments.

Example

In a product development team, a T-shaped designer may have deep skills in user interface (UI) design but also understand basic coding, project management, and user research. This allows them to work effectively with developers, product managers, and researchers. Their broad awareness ensures smoother collaboration, fewer silos, and more user-centred results.

Why It Works

T-shaped individuals bridge gaps between departments, enabling faster communication and better problem-solving. Their depth ensures high-quality work in their domain, while their breadth allows them to appreciate and integrate contributions from other experts. This reduces friction and promotes innovation, especially in cross-functional teams.

It also aligns well with today's fast-changing world, where versatility and collaboration often outperform isolated expertise.

How It Works

T-shaped people contribute value in two key ways:

- **Specialization**: They own specific tasks and bring mastery to the table.

- **Collaboration**: They engage in interdisciplinary conversations, grasp context quickly, and support adjacent functions when needed.

This model thrives in environments that reward teamwork, curiosity, and continuous learning. Employers often assess breadth through communication skills, emotional intelligence, and openness to feedback.

Application

The T-shaped model is used in **hiring**, **team design**, and **personal development**. Tech firms, creative agencies, and startups often seek T-shaped professionals to build agile, collaborative teams. Educational institutions also promote T-shaped development through liberal arts foundations combined with technical majors.

Key Insights

- Deep expertise remains essential—but it's not enough on its own.

- Breadth fosters empathy, adaptability, and collaboration.

- T-shaped individuals thrive in multidisciplinary environments.

- The model encourages continuous learning and cross-skill development.

- Teams of T-shaped people are more resilient and innovative.

In essence, the T-shaped model offers a powerful lens for building balanced individuals and high-functioning, future-ready teams.

57. Open-Loop vs. Closed-Loop

The **Open-Loop vs. Closed-Loop** mental model comes from control theory and systems thinking. It describes how systems manage feedback and make adjustments. Understanding this model is critical for decision-making, learning, and process optimization.

Theoretical Basis

- An **open-loop system** acts without using feedback. It follows a set of instructions or actions without checking if the desired outcome was achieved. It assumes things will go as planned.

- A **closed-loop system**, in contrast, includes feedback. It continuously monitors outputs and adjusts inputs based on actual results to maintain or improve performance.

This concept is used in engineering, biology, business, and behaviour—anywhere outcomes depend on iterative learning and adaptation.

Example

Consider a thermostat:

- **Open-loop**: A heater turns on for 30 minutes regardless of the room temperature. It may overheat or underheat the room.

- **Closed-loop**: A thermostat senses the room temperature and turns the heater on or off to maintain a set point. It self-corrects based on real-time data.

In human behaviour:

- Open-loop thinking: Setting a New Year's goal to "get fit" but never tracking progress.

- Closed-loop thinking: Setting the same goal but tracking workouts, adjusting routines, and responding to outcomes—like soreness or energy levels.

Why It Works

Closed-loop systems work better because they **learn from feedback**. Real-world situations are often unpredictable. Relying on fixed plans (open-loop) can lead to missed targets or unintended outcomes. Feedback allows for course correction, improvement, and resilience.

Open-loop systems are faster and simpler but vulnerable to error. They work best in highly predictable or low-stakes environments.

How It Works

Closed-loop thinking operates through **measurement, feedback**, and **adjustment**:

1. A goal or desired state is defined.

2. The actual outcome is measured.

3. A comparison is made between the two.

4. Adjustments are made based on the difference.

It's a cycle of constant refinement, often visualized as a feedback loop.

Open-loop thinking, by contrast, follows a one-way path: input → action → output, with no evaluation or revision.

Application

This model applies broadly:

- **In business**: Closed-loop systems drive customer feedback, agile development, and performance reviews.

- **In education**: Students learn better when they receive timely feedback and revise work accordingly.

- **In leadership**: Effective leaders listen, reflect, and adjust rather than acting blindly.

Key Insights

- Feedback is the engine of improvement.

- Closed-loop systems outperform open-loop ones in dynamic environments.

- Measuring outcomes is critical to learning and success.

- Mistakes in open-loop systems often go undetected.

- Awareness of loop type enhances better decision-making.

In essence, life works better when we listen, learn, and adjust—closed-loop thinking is how we evolve.

58. Bullwhip Effect

The **Bullwhip Effect** is a supply chain phenomenon where small fluctuations in customer demand cause increasingly larger variations in orders and inventory levels up the supply chain. Named for the way a small flick of the wrist can create a large motion at the end of a bullwhip, this model reveals how minor shifts at the consumer level can lead to major disruptions for suppliers, manufacturers, and distributors.

Theoretical Basis

The Bullwhip Effect arises due to delays in communication, overreactions to demand changes, batch ordering, price fluctuations, and a lack of transparency across the supply chain. It was first observed in the 1960s and gained prominence through studies by Procter & Gamble and later MIT researchers, who showed how even predictable demand (like for diapers) could cause wild swings in manufacturing orders due to poor coordination.

Example

Suppose a grocery store sees a 10% spike in toilet paper sales. Interpreting this as a lasting trend, they order 20% more from the wholesaler. The wholesaler, noticing the increase, orders 30% more from the manufacturer. The manufacturer ramps up production and inventories in anticipation of a surge. When consumer demand returns to normal, the entire supply chain is left with excess stock, wasted resources, and financial losses.

Why It Works (or Fails)

The Bullwhip Effect persists because each player in the supply chain acts independently, often without full visibility into actual consumer demand. Decisions are made based on perceived demand rather than real-time data, leading to overproduction or stockouts. Fear of running out of stock, long lead times, and volume discounts further magnify the problem.

How It Works

The effect is driven by four key factors:

1. **Demand signal processing** – Misinterpreting customer demand.

2. **Order batching** – Placing infrequent, large orders to save on costs.

3. **Price variations** – Promotions and discounts leading to bulk buying.

4. **Rationing and gaming** – Inflated orders placed during perceived shortages.

Each action amplifies the distortion of demand as it travels upstream, creating inefficiencies, higher costs, and customer dissatisfaction.

Application

The Bullwhip Effect is crucial in **supply chain management**, **retail**, **logistics**, and **manufacturing**. Companies mitigate it by using **real-time data**, **collaborative forecasting**, **just-in-time (JIT) inventory**, and **information sharing** across partners.

Key Insights

- Local decisions can have system-wide consequences.

- Lack of transparency amplifies inefficiency.

- Coordination and communication are critical to system stability.

- Demand forecasting must be shared and collaborative.

- Technology (like ERP and AI) can reduce distortion.

Understanding the Bullwhip Effect helps organizations build more responsive, resilient, and efficient supply chains—essential in today's volatile global markets.

59. Six Sigma

Six Sigma is a data-driven methodology and mental model for process improvement that aims to reduce defects and variability in operations. Developed by **Motorola** in the 1980s and later popularized by **General Electric**, Six Sigma provides a structured, disciplined approach to achieving operational excellence and delivering consistent, high-quality results.

Theoretical Basis

At its core, Six Sigma seeks to improve processes by identifying and eliminating the causes of defects and minimizing variability. The term "Six Sigma" refers to a statistical concept: achieving a process that produces fewer than 3.4 defects per million opportunities (DPMO). This level of quality represents near perfection.

Six Sigma is built around the **DMAIC framework**:

1. **Define** – Identify the problem and project goals.

2. **Measure** – Gather data and establish current performance.

3. **Analyse** – Identify root causes of defects or inefficiencies.

4. **Improve** – Develop and implement solutions.

5. **Control** – Sustain improvements and prevent regression.

Example

A manufacturing company experiences frequent defects in its product packaging. Using Six Sigma, the team defines the defect (misaligned labels), measures how often it occurs, analyses the root cause (machine calibration issues), improves the process by updating calibration protocols, and controls the new process with routine checks. As a result, defect rates drop significantly, saving time and cost.

Why It Works

Six Sigma works because it relies on **evidence-based decision-making**, **process standardization**, and **root cause analysis**. By focusing on data rather than assumptions, it avoids trial-and-error approaches and ensures changes address the real problems. It also fosters a culture of continuous improvement and accountability.

How It Works

It leverages **statistical tools**, **control charts**, **process mapping**, and **hypothesis testing** to detect variation and inefficiency. Teams trained in Six Sigma (often categorized as Yellow, Green, or Black Belts) use this toolkit to systematically solve problems. The structured DMAIC cycle ensures that each step is thoughtfully planned, executed, and monitored.

Six Sigma also incorporates customer-centric thinking by emphasizing **CTQs** (Critical to Quality factors)—the features most important to the customer.

Application

Six Sigma is used across industries: in **manufacturing** for quality control, **healthcare** for reducing patient wait times, **finance** for error-free transactions, and **software** for improving code quality. It is also applied in service industries to streamline workflows and improve customer experience.

Key Insights

- Quality improvement requires data, not guesswork.
- Small changes, when measured and controlled, create lasting impact.
- Processes, not people, are often the source of defects.
- Standardization and feedback loops ensure sustainability.
- Culture and training are key to long-term success.

Six Sigma is not just a toolset but a mindset—focused on excellence through precision, clarity, and continuous learning.

60. Minimum Viable Product (MVP)

The **Minimum Viable Product (MVP)** is a mental model and product development strategy rooted in the **Lean Startup** methodology, popularized by **Eric Ries**. The MVP is a simplified version of a product that contains just enough core features to be deployed and tested by early users, with the goal of validating assumptions and learning quickly with minimal risk and investment.

Theoretical Basis

The core idea behind the MVP is to avoid building a full-featured product based on untested assumptions. Instead, by launching a basic version early, teams can gather real-world feedback and iterate. This model aligns with principles of **experimentation**, **validated learning**, and **agility**—focusing on building what people actually need, not what we assume they want.

It's better to test a hypothesis quickly than to spend months building a product that fails in the market due to misaligned features or flawed assumptions.

Example

Consider Dropbox's early MVP. Before building the full file-sharing platform, the founders created a simple explainer video demonstrating how the product would work. They shared it with a tech-savvy audience and observed huge interest and sign-ups—validating demand without writing a full line of code. Only after confirming user interest did they build the actual product.

Why It Works

The MVP model works because it minimizes **waste**—in time, money, and effort—by focusing only on what's necessary to learn. Instead of guessing or assuming market fit, teams test real user behaviour. This reduces the risk of failure, accelerates feedback loops, and encourages a culture of learning and iteration.

By starting small, teams stay adaptable and can pivot based on what they learn.

How It Works

MVPs are built by identifying the **core problem** the product is solving and creating the simplest version that delivers value. Teams then:

1. Launch the MVP to early adopters.

2. Gather usage data and feedback.

3. Iterate based on what works or doesn't.

4. Gradually add or modify features based on validated learning.

The goal isn't perfection—it's insight.

Application

MVP thinking is essential in **startups**, **product design**, **software development**, and **innovation teams** within large companies. It's also used in **marketing experiments**, **course creation**, or even **event planning**—anywhere assumptions can be tested before full-scale execution.

Key Insights

- MVPs reduce risk by testing ideas early.

- Learning from users is more valuable than perfecting guesses.

- Speed and adaptability outperform perfection in uncertain environments.

- Every product starts with a hypothesis—validate it quickly.

- MVPs are about progress, not polish.

In short, the MVP model helps turn bold ideas into reality with minimal risk and maximum learning.

Biological and Evolutionary Models:

61. Survival of the Fittest

Survival of the Fittest is a foundational mental model derived from **Charles Darwin's theory of natural selection**, though the phrase itself was coined by philosopher **Herbert Spencer**. It describes how, in a competitive environment, individuals, systems, or ideas that are best adapted to current conditions are more likely to endure and thrive, while those less adapted tend to fail or disappear.

Theoretical Basis

In biology, "fitness" doesn't mean strength, but rather suitability to a given environment. Traits that enhance survival and reproduction are more likely to be passed on. Over time, species evolve to reflect the pressures and constraints of their surroundings. This model can be applied not only to biology but also to **business, technology, culture**, and **personal development**—any system where adaptation and competition drive success.

Example

In the business world, think of companies like **Blockbuster** and **Netflix**. Blockbuster failed to adapt to the digital streaming trend, clinging to physical rentals. Netflix, by contrast, evolved its model—first mailing DVDs, then moving to streaming, and now producing original content.

Netflix was "fitter" in the changing technological environment and therefore survived and flourished.

Why It Works

This model works because environments are always changing—economically, socially, ecologically. Those who adapt, innovate, or evolve in response to these changes increase their chances of success. The model emphasizes **resilience**, **flexibility**, and **relevance** as keys to longevity.

On the flip side, failure to adapt often leads to extinction—whether it's a species, business, idea, or individual skill set.

How It Works

Survival of the Fittest operates through **selection pressure**. These pressures—competition, customer preference, regulatory change, or climate—act like filters. Entities that meet or exceed those demands continue on; others fall away.

In organizational terms, the "fittest" company may not be the biggest, but the one that best fits customer needs, navigates uncertainty, and innovates consistently. In personal development, those who continuously learn and adapt are more likely to succeed over time.

Application

This model is used in **business strategy, evolutionary algorithms, product development**, and **career planning**. Entrepreneurs apply it when pivoting business models based on user feedback. Individuals apply it by updating skills to stay relevant in changing job markets.

Key Insights

- Adaptability is more important than raw strength or size.

- External conditions determine what traits or strategies are "fit."

- Success is dynamic—what works now may not work tomorrow.

- Feedback and iteration are essential for long-term survival.

- Complacency is a silent killer in evolving systems.

Ultimately, **Survival of the Fittest** reminds us that in life, business, and nature, adaptability isn't optional—it's everything.

62. Mutualism

Mutualism is a mental model rooted in **ecology**, describing interactions between organisms where **both parties benefit** from the relationship. Unlike parasitism or competition, mutualism is **cooperative**, creating **shared value** that enhances survival, resilience, or performance.

This concept extends beyond biology and is highly applicable in business, partnerships, personal relationships, and systems thinking.

Theoretical Basis

In biology, mutualism occurs when two species develop a symbiotic relationship that supports their mutual success. Classic examples include:

- **Bees and flowers**: Bees get nectar for food; flowers get pollinated.

- **Humans and gut bacteria**: Bacteria help digest food; humans provide a stable environment.

This interdependence often leads to **coevolution**, where both species adapt to optimize the relationship over time. In broader systems, mutualism implies that collaboration— when designed well—can produce more value than isolated effort.

Example

Consider the strategic alliance between **Apple and app developers**. Apple provides a platform (iOS) and access to millions of users. Developers, in turn, create apps that enhance the value of Apple's devices. Apple earns from the App Store; developers gain exposure and revenue. Both thrive more than they would alone.

Why It Works

Mutualism works because it leverages **complementary strengths** and aligns **incentives**. When both sides benefit, there's motivation to maintain and strengthen the relationship. It creates **positive-sum outcomes**, where cooperation produces more than either party could achieve independently.

Unlike competition, which often produces winners and losers, mutualism fosters sustainable growth and long-term partnerships.

How It Works

It functions through **reciprocity, alignment,** and **feedback loops**:

1. **Reciprocity** – Each party gives and receives value.

2. **Alignment** – Shared goals or interests reduce friction.

3. **Feedback loops** – Ongoing interaction improves the relationship over time.

Successful mutualism depends on **trust**, **transparency**, and the ability to adapt. If one party begins to overexploit the other, the balance breaks, and mutualism can degrade into exploitation or dependency.

Application

Mutualism applies across disciplines:

- **Business**: Brand collaborations, joint ventures, and supply chain partnerships.

- **Technology**: Open-source communities where developers contribute and benefit collectively.

- **Personal life**: Friendships or partnerships where support flows both ways.

Leaders and teams who think in mutualistic terms focus on **value creation**, not just value extraction.

Key Insights

- Mutual benefit creates more resilient, enduring systems.

- Aligned incentives lead to cooperation and growth.

- Healthy mutualism requires maintenance and balance.

- Positive relationships outperform transactional ones over time.

- Win-win thinking is a strategic advantage in a connected world.

In essence, mutualism teaches us that success isn't a solo act—it thrives on connection, contribution, and shared value.

63. Coevolution

Coevolution is a mental model from evolutionary biology describing how two or more species, systems, or entities evolve in response to each other over time. Rather than evolving in isolation, they shape each other's development, creating a feedback loop of mutual influence and adaptation. This concept extends far beyond biology into business, technology, relationships, and ecosystems thinking.

Theoretical Basis

In nature, coevolution is observed when the evolution of one species directly affects the evolution of another. This can be **mutualistic** (beneficial to both), **antagonistic** (competitive or adversarial), or **commensal** (one benefits, the other is neutral).

Examples include:

- **Bees and flowering plants** evolving in tandem for pollination.

- **Predators and prey** evolving better hunting and defence strategies.

- **Parasites and hosts** adapting to outmanoeuvre each other.

In human systems, coevolution appears wherever interactions create reciprocal change over time.

Example

Consider the coevolution of **smartphones and social behaviour**. As smartphone capabilities expanded, social habits changed—people began communicating differently, relying on mobile apps for everything from news to relationships. In turn, tech companies adapted their products to reflect these new habits (e.g., push notifications, social feeds, voice assistants). Society and technology are coevolving, shaping one another continuously.

Why It Works

Coevolution works because systems don't exist in isolation. They interact, influence, and adapt in real time. When two entities are closely connected—biologically, economically, or socially—the success of one becomes dependent on how well it responds to the changes in the other.

This model helps explain why simple, one-sided solutions often fail in complex environments. It emphasizes the importance of responsiveness and interdependence.

How It Works

Coevolution is driven by **feedback loops**:

1. One entity changes (adapts, innovates, evolves).

2. The other responds to that change.

3. This response triggers further adaptation in the first.

4. The cycle continues, gradually transforming both.

These cycles can be slow (as in natural evolution) or rapid (as in tech and culture).

Application

Coevolution is crucial in:

- **Business ecosystems** (e.g., platforms like Amazon evolving with sellers).

- **Technology and user behaviour**.

- **International relations**, where countries influence each other's policies.

- **Organizational design**, where teams adapt alongside their environment.

Leaders, designers, and strategists use coevolution to anticipate how changes in one area will ripple across others—and how to adapt in turn.

Key Insights

- No system evolves alone—everything is interconnected.

- Adaptive success depends on mutual responsiveness.

- Long-term change is often reciprocal, not unilateral.

- Innovation triggers counter-innovation.

- Understanding coevolution builds strategic foresight.

Coevolution shows us that thriving in complex systems means evolving *with* the world—not against it.

64. Genetic Drift

Genetic Drift is a concept from evolutionary biology that explains how random chance—not just natural selection—can influence the evolution of populations. It describes how allele frequencies (variations of a gene) can shift over time due to random sampling, especially in small populations. Unlike natural selection, which is adaptive and driven by environmental pressures, genetic drift is **non-directional** and **random**, yet it can still produce significant long-term effects.

Theoretical Basis

Genetic drift occurs when certain traits become more or less common not because they're more advantageous, but simply due to **random events**. Over generations, these random changes can lead to traits becoming fixed (100% common) or lost (0% occurrence) in a population.

Two common types of genetic drift include:

- **Bottleneck effect** – When a population sharply reduces in size (e.g., due to disaster), the surviving gene pool may not represent the original population.

- **Founder effect** – When a small group splits off to form a new population, their limited genetic makeup can shape the future population in a unique, random direction.

Example

Imagine a small island with a population of 10 lizards—half green, half brown. A random storm kills six, and purely by chance, five of the survivors are green. The green allele becomes dominant, not because it's more fit, but due to chance. Over time, brown lizards may disappear entirely from the gene pool—even if their trait was equally viable.

Why It Works

Genetic drift "works" (i.e., has an effect) because in small samples, **random events have outsized impacts**. The fewer the individuals in a population, the more likely that statistical fluctuations will drastically shape outcomes. Unlike selection, drift doesn't require environmental pressures or competitive advantages—just randomness.

This model is valuable because it reminds us that not all change is purposeful or directional. Sometimes, systems evolve by **chance**, not merit.

How It Works

Genetic drift operates through **random sampling error** in each generation:

1. Individuals reproduce.

2. Offspring receive a random subset of genes.

3. Over time, certain genes may disappear or dominate due to chance.

4. In isolated or small populations, this effect amplifies.

Application

Beyond biology, genetic drift is useful in **economics**, **culture**, **business**, and **innovation**. For instance:

- In startups, random early successes (or failures) can disproportionately influence trajectory.

- In culture, certain ideas or trends become dominant not because they're better, but because of early adoption by influencers or random visibility.

Key Insights

- Not all outcomes are due to merit; chance plays a powerful role.

- Small systems are especially vulnerable to randomness.

- Early events can disproportionately shape future trajectories.

- Drift can lead to fragility or unexpected dominance.

- Understanding randomness helps temper overconfidence in outcomes.

In essence, **Genetic Drift** highlights the invisible hand of chance in shaping systems—and the humility required to recognize it.

65. Mimicry

Mimicry is a mental model derived from evolutionary biology, where one organism evolves to resemble another for survival advantages. This resemblance can be visual, behavioural, or chemical. While it's a biological concept at its core, mimicry also applies broadly to human behaviour, marketing, strategy, and innovation—anywhere imitation can be used to gain a benefit or avoid harm.

Theoretical Basis

In nature, mimicry serves various purposes:

- **Batesian mimicry**: A harmless species imitates a harmful one to avoid predators (e.g., a non-venomous snake mimicking a venomous one).

- **Müllerian mimicry**: Two harmful species evolve similar warning signals, reinforcing avoidance behaviour in predators.

- **Aggressive mimicry**: Predators or parasites mimic harmless entities to deceive their prey (e.g., anglerfish using a lure that looks like prey).

The underlying principle is **deception or reinforcement through similarity**. Mimicry takes advantage of other organisms' perception and decision-making processes for strategic benefit.

Example

In the business world, **store-brand products** often mimic the packaging of leading brands. A supermarket's generic cereal might copy the colour scheme, font, and box shape of a popular brand to create the illusion of similarity in quality. Consumers may choose the cheaper mimic based on visual cues, even if they're unaware of the substitution.

Why It Works

Mimicry works because **humans and animals make decisions based on patterns and assumptions**. When something appears familiar, safe, or effective, it tends to be trusted or avoided based on prior associations. Mimicry leverages these mental shortcuts—what psychology calls **heuristics**—to influence behaviour without requiring rational analysis.

It's a fast, efficient way to benefit from established signals, reputations, or deterrents.

How It Works

Mimicry functions by:

1. **Identifying an advantageous target** to imitate (e.g., a successful product, behaviour, or trait).

2. **Replicating key signals or attributes** that observers associate with value or threat.

3. **Triggering an automatic response** based on the mimic's resemblance to the original.

Whether in nature or strategy, success depends on how closely the mimic aligns with the target and how perceptive the observer is.

Application

Mimicry is applied in:

- **Marketing**: New brands imitate design cues of market leaders.

- **Cybersecurity**: Fake websites mimic legitimate ones to trick users.

- **Social behaviour**: People unconsciously mimic posture, speech, or tone to build rapport.

- **Innovation**: Startups mimic successful business models with tweaks (a practice known as "cloning" in tech).

Key Insights

- Mimicry is a powerful shortcut to influence perception.

- It thrives on pattern recognition and assumptions.

- Effective mimicry requires subtlety and timing.

- Mimicry can be defensive (avoidance), offensive (deception), or cooperative (alignment).

- It reveals how perception often outweighs reality in decision-making.

In short, mimicry reminds us that **similarity can be strategy**, and that appearances—rightly or wrongly—shape outcomes.

66. Ecosystem Thinking

Ecosystem Thinking is a mental model that encourages viewing systems—whether in nature, business, or society—not as isolated parts, but as **interconnected networks** of entities that affect and depend on one another. It originates from **ecology**, where ecosystems are dynamic environments of organisms, resources, and relationships constantly interacting to maintain balance and adapt to change.

Theoretical Basis

In an ecological ecosystem, plants, animals, microorganisms, water, soil, and climate all form a self-regulating system. Each component plays a role, and changes in one part ripple across the whole. Similarly, in human systems—like a business or digital platform—customers, partners, suppliers, regulators, and competitors form an interdependent web.

Ecosystem Thinking challenges linear, siloed problem-solving by promoting a **systems-based approach**. Instead of focusing solely on internal goals, it emphasizes understanding relationships, feedback loops, and long-term consequences.

Example

Consider **Apple's ecosystem**: its hardware (iPhones, iPads), software (iOS), services (iCloud, Apple Music), and third-party apps all work seamlessly together. Developers, accessory makers, and users form an ecosystem where each participant benefits from others. Apple doesn't just sell products—it curates and nurtures a thriving digital environment, making it harder for users to switch and easier to grow value collaboratively.

Why It Works

Ecosystem Thinking works because it mirrors **reality**— where few things exist in isolation. It allows decision-makers to see **second-order effects**, anticipate unintended consequences, and uncover **opportunities for synergy**. In adaptive, fast-moving environments, those who think in networks rather than silos are more likely to thrive.

It also promotes **resilience**. If one node or partner weakens, the system can adjust through other connections, much like natural ecosystems recover from disturbances.

How It Works

Ecosystem Thinking involves:

1. **Mapping the system**: Identify all actors, connections, and dependencies.

2. **Understanding incentives**: Know what each participant gains and risks.

3. **Recognizing interdependence**: No part succeeds in isolation.

4. **Designing for co-evolution**: Encourage feedback and continuous alignment.

It also encourages **value co-creation**—where value emerges not from controlling the system, but from enabling others within it to flourish.

Application

This model is widely used in:

- **Platform businesses** (e.g., Amazon, Airbnb)

- **Urban planning** and **sustainable development**

- **Healthcare systems** (linking providers, patients, payers, technology)

- **Innovation networks** and **open-source communities**

Key Insights

- Success is increasingly collaborative, not competitive.

- Value flows through relationships, not just transactions.

- Ecosystems thrive through alignment, adaptation, and diversity.

- Systems must be nurtured, not controlled.

- Thinking in ecosystems builds foresight and long-term strategy.

In essence, **Ecosystem Thinking** helps us design smarter, more sustainable solutions by recognizing that everything is connected.

67. R/K Selection Theory

R/K Selection Theory is a concept from **evolutionary biology** that explains how different species adopt different reproductive strategies based on environmental conditions. Developed in the 1960s and rooted in population ecology, the model helps us understand trade-offs between **quantity and quality** in reproduction—and can be applied more broadly to decision-making, strategy, and resource allocation.

Theoretical Basis

The theory categorizes organisms along a spectrum:

- **r-selected species** (from the *r* in the growth rate equation) prioritize **high reproduction rates**. They produce many offspring, invest little in each, and thrive in **unstable or unpredictable environments**. Think: insects, weeds, or bacteria.

- **K-selected species** (from the *K* for carrying capacity) invest in **fewer offspring** with more parental care. They succeed in **stable, competitive environments** where quality matters more than quantity. Examples include elephants, humans, and whales.

The r/K model illustrates the trade-off between **speed and sustainability**, **quantity and investment**, and **short-term gain vs. long-term survival**.

Example

Consider two business strategies:

- A startup rapidly launching multiple products with minimal investment to test the market—an **r-strategy**. It relies on speed, flexibility, and high trial volume.

- A luxury brand spending years developing one high-end product with strong customer service and a long lifecycle—a **K-strategy**, focused on depth, quality, and brand equity.

Each approach aligns with different environments: one rewards fast iteration, the other long-term trust.

Why It Works

The model works because different environments demand different survival strategies. In chaotic or untested spaces, r-strategies thrive by flooding the zone and maximizing the odds that *something* sticks. In mature or saturated markets, K-strategies win by offering stability, reliability, and depth of value.

This mental model encourages **situational awareness** and helps avoid mismatched strategies.

How It Works

R/K Selection Theory works by:

1. Assessing environmental stability and competition.

2. Choosing a reproduction (or output) strategy: quantity (r) or quality (K).

3. Allocating resources accordingly—either toward fast replication or long-term development.

Importantly, these aren't fixed identities—entities may shift strategies as environments change.

Application

This model applies to:

- **Business**: MVPs vs. premium product development.

- **Marketing**: Mass outreach vs. targeted relationship building.

- **Education**: Broad course exposure vs. deep specialization.

- **Career strategy**: Job-hopping for exploration vs. mastery in a single domain.

Key Insights

- No single strategy fits all contexts—fit matters.

- Resource allocation reflects your underlying strategy.

- Early environments shape long-term outcomes.

- Speed (r) and depth (K) are trade-offs, not opposites.

- Strategic adaptation is critical as conditions evolve.

In essence, **R/K Selection Theory** teaches that success depends not just on effort—but on choosing the right strategy for the right environment.

68. Homeostasis

Homeostasis is a foundational concept from **biology** that describes a system's ability to maintain **internal stability** despite external changes. It refers to the dynamic balance organisms or systems preserve through continuous self-regulation. While it originally explained how living organisms regulate temperature, pH, or blood sugar, **homeostasis** applies far beyond biology—to psychology, organizations, economics, and complex systems.

Theoretical Basis

From the Greek *"homeo"* (same) and *"stasis"* (standing still), homeostasis describes how systems detect deviations from a desired state and activate mechanisms to return to equilibrium. This process is governed by **feedback loops**, particularly **negative feedback**—a corrective response that counteracts the disturbance.

For example, if your body temperature rises, mechanisms like sweating cool it down. If it drops, you shiver to generate heat. The body doesn't seek a rigid state but a **dynamic equilibrium**, adjusting as needed to remain functional.

Example

In economics, central banks maintain **monetary homeostasis**. When inflation rises, interest rates are increased to cool spending. When the economy slows, rates are lowered to stimulate demand. These regulatory actions keep the economic system within an acceptable range, preventing extreme booms or busts.

Similarly, in personal life, people have a psychological "set point" for happiness or stress. After major changes— positive or negative—they often return to a baseline emotional state, illustrating **emotional homeostasis**.

Why It Works

Homeostasis works because systems require **stability** to function effectively. Without regulation, small disturbances could spiral into system failure. The feedback mechanisms in homeostatic systems make them **resilient**, capable of adapting to change without losing core integrity.

In nature and organizations alike, survival often depends on the ability to sense change and respond appropriately— without overcorrecting or resisting change entirely.

How It Works

Homeostatic systems follow a basic loop:

1. **Sensor** detects deviation from the set point.

2. **Control centre** interprets the signal and decides on a response.

3. **Effector** initiates the correction.

4. System returns to baseline—unless conditions change again.

These loops run constantly and adjust automatically, allowing for rapid, decentralized regulation.

Application

This model is relevant in:

- **Health**: Managing stress, sleep, or diet.

- **Business**: Balancing innovation with core processes.

- **Technology**: Thermostats, software performance management.

- **Society**: Legal systems and checks-and-balances.

Understanding homeostasis helps leaders design systems that are **adaptive but stable**, capable of absorbing shocks without collapse.

Key Insights

- Stability comes from feedback, not rigidity.

- Small disruptions are inevitable—what matters is the response.

- Systems thrive when they balance flexibility and control.

- Overcorrection can be as harmful as no correction.

- True resilience lies in **self-regulation**, not resistance.

In short, **Homeostasis** reminds us that intelligent balance—not perfection—is the secret to sustained function and health in any system.

69. Critical Mass in Biology

Critical Mass in biology refers to the **minimum threshold** of individuals, resources, or conditions necessary for a **biological system or population to sustain itself and grow**. Below this threshold, the system risks collapse; above it, it can expand and thrive. While the term originates in physics (nuclear reactions), in biology it applies to populations, ecosystems, and cellular processes where survival or success depends on reaching and maintaining a certain scale.

Theoretical Basis

In population biology, critical mass is closely tied to the **Allee effect**—a principle that describes how populations may fail to grow, or even decline, when they fall below a certain number. Reasons include:

- Difficulty finding mates
- Reduced genetic diversity
- Poor cooperation or defence
- Vulnerability to predators or environmental shifts

The concept is not limited to population size—it also applies to **cell growth, immune responses, and microbial colonies**, where a certain density or coordination level is essential to trigger collective behaviours or biological functions.

Example

In microbial biology, **quorum sensing** in bacteria illustrates this model. Bacteria release signalling molecules into their environment. When the bacterial population reaches a critical density, the concentration of these molecules crosses a threshold, triggering coordinated behaviours such as bioluminescence, virulence, or biofilm formation. Without enough bacteria (i.e., below critical mass), these functions never activate.

Similarly, a small population of endangered animals may decline toward extinction even if their habitat is protected, simply because they fall below critical breeding or interaction thresholds.

Why It Works

Critical mass matters because many biological processes rely on **collective interactions**. Below a certain point, key functions like reproduction, defence, or signal coordination cannot operate effectively. Reaching critical mass enables **network effects**, synergy, and system-level behaviours that isolated individuals cannot achieve.

This model underscores that in biology, **more isn't always better—but too little is often fatal**.

How It Works

The process typically follows this pattern:

1. Individuals or components interact minimally at low density.

2. As numbers increase, interaction rates rise.

3. At a tipping point (critical mass), system-wide behaviours emerge.

4. Feedback loops reinforce growth or stability.

This threshold is often non-linear, meaning small increases near the tipping point can lead to exponential change.

Application

The model applies in:

- **Conservation biology**: Managing species at risk of extinction.

- **Cancer research**: Understanding when tumour cells become self-sustaining.

- **Epidemiology**: Disease outbreaks occur once a pathogen spreads beyond a critical mass of hosts.

- **Synthetic biology**: Engineering cells to perform group tasks only above a population threshold.

Key Insights

- Systems often need a minimum scale to function or persist.

- Below critical mass, decline accelerates.

- Thresholds can trigger emergent behaviour.

- Growth strategies must consider scale and timing.

- Collaboration and density often unlock new capabilities.

In short, **Critical Mass** in biology teaches us that **survival and function often depend not just on presence, but on scale**—a vital insight for managing both natural and engineered life systems.

70. Life History Theory

Life History Theory is an evolutionary biology framework that explains how organisms allocate their limited energy and resources across the key stages of life: **growth, reproduction, and survival**. The theory posits that life strategies evolve based on environmental pressures, shaping how species time and balance decisions like when to mature, how often to reproduce, and how much to invest in offspring.

Theoretical Basis

Life History Theory assumes that energy is finite, and organisms face **trade-offs**. Investing more in one area (e.g., reproduction) often means sacrificing another (e.g., longevity or parental care). These trade-offs are shaped by natural selection to maximize fitness in a given ecological context.

Species evolve along a **spectrum** between two broad strategies:

- **Fast life history (r-strategy)**: Early reproduction, many offspring, low parental investment, short lifespan. Adapted for **unstable environments** with high mortality.

- **Slow life history (K-strategy)**: Later reproduction, fewer offspring, high parental investment, longer lifespan. Suited to **stable environments** where competition is high and survival is more predictable.

Example

Consider **mice** and **elephants**. Mice mature quickly, reproduce prolifically, and live only a few years—classic fast strategy. Elephants, on the other hand, take years to mature, have few offspring with significant parental care, and live for decades—a slow strategy.

Humans also show life history variation. In resource-scarce or high-risk environments, people may favour earlier reproduction and shorter planning horizons. In stable settings, individuals tend to delay reproduction, pursue education, and invest more in fewer children.

Why It Works

Life History Theory works because it reflects **adaptive responses** to environmental constraints. Organisms that match their reproductive and survival strategies to their ecological conditions are more likely to pass on their genes. It reveals how evolution doesn't aim for perfection, but for **fitness trade-offs** that suit the context.

How It Works

The model functions through:

1. **Environmental cues**: Mortality risk, food availability, predation, and competition shape development.

2. **Developmental timing**: Organisms "decide" (genetically or behaviourally) how quickly to grow and reproduce.

3. **Resource allocation**: Energy is divided among competing needs—growth, reproduction, maintenance.

Changes in these variables trigger shifts along the fast–slow continuum.

Application

Beyond biology, Life History Theory is applied in:

- **Psychology**: Explaining differences in risk-taking, parenting, and time preferences.

- **Sociology**: Understanding how economic conditions influence reproductive behaviour.

- **Public health**: Addressing early-life stress and its effects on development and lifespan.

Key Insights

- Energy trade-offs drive biological and behavioural strategies.

- There's no one-size-fits-all approach—context dictates the best strategy.

- Early-life environments shape life trajectory.

- Fast strategies emphasize quantity; slow strategies emphasize quality.

- Evolution favors flexibility, not just endurance.

In essence, **Life History Theory** teaches that life strategies are about **timing, trade-offs, and tuning behaviour to context**—a dynamic dance between survival and reproduction shaped by our environments.

Philosophical and Ethical Models:

71. Moral Relativism

Moral Relativism is a philosophical and ethical framework that posits **morality is not absolute**, but rather **context-dependent**. According to this model, moral judgments and ethical standards are shaped by **culture, history, social norms, and individual perspectives**, rather than by any universal or objective moral law.

Theoretical Basis

Moral Relativism stands in contrast to **moral absolutism**, which claims that certain actions are universally right or wrong regardless of context. Relativism holds that **what is considered "moral" varies across societies and eras**, and that understanding morality requires recognizing this variation.

There are two main types:

- **Cultural Relativism**: Morality is defined by cultural context—what's right in one culture may be wrong in another.

- **Individual Relativism (Subjectivism)**: Moral beliefs are based on personal perspectives and may differ from person to person.

The model is rooted in anthropology, sociology, and postmodern philosophy, notably influenced by thinkers like **Franz Boas**, **Michel Foucault**, and **Richard Rorty**.

Example

Take the practice of **arranged marriage**. In some cultures, it is a respected tradition associated with family honour and social stability. In others, it may be seen as restricting personal freedom. Moral Relativism doesn't claim one view is "correct," but rather that both are **valid within their cultural frameworks**.

Another example is attitudes toward **alcohol**. What is permissible in one country may be morally condemned in another based on religion, law, or tradition.

Why It Works

Moral Relativism works because it promotes **cultural sensitivity**, **tolerance**, and **open-mindedness**. By recognizing that others' moral codes arise from different experiences and histories, it encourages dialogue rather than judgment. It also acknowledges the **complexity of human behaviour** and avoids the oversimplification of universal moral rules.

In a diverse and interconnected world, relativism helps reduce ethnocentrism and fosters peaceful coexistence among differing worldviews.

How It Works

Relativism operates through:

1. **Contextual analysis**: Understanding values within the environment that shaped them.

2. **Non-imposition**: Avoiding the enforcement of one's moral beliefs on others.

3. **Pluralism**: Accepting multiple moral systems as legitimate.

It is less concerned with establishing "truth" and more focused on **interpretation and coexistence**.

Application

Moral Relativism is relevant in:

- **International relations**: Navigating legal and ethical norms across countries.

- **Anthropology**: Studying cultural practices without judgment.

- **Business ethics**: Managing global teams with different value systems.

- **Conflict resolution**: Mediating disputes rooted in moral differences.

Key Insights

- Morality is not universal—it is shaped by context.

- Understanding others requires suspending personal bias.

- Ethical diversity is a natural outcome of human cultures.

- Absolutism can lead to intolerance; relativism fosters dialogue.

- Coexistence requires empathy, not uniformity.

In essence, **Moral Relativism** teaches that to truly understand others, we must first recognize the lens through which we see the world is only one among many.

72. Utilitarianism

Utilitarianism is a moral and philosophical framework that proposes the **best action is the one that maximizes overall happiness or well-being**. Rooted in consequentialism, utilitarianism judges actions based on their **outcomes**, not intentions. It is one of the most influential ethical models in Western thought, developed most prominently by **Jeremy Bentham** and **John Stuart Mill** in the 18th and 19th centuries.

Theoretical Basis

At its core, utilitarianism is built on the **principle of utility**—often summed up as "the greatest good for the greatest number." Bentham proposed that we should calculate pleasure and pain (hedonistic calculus) when making decisions. Mill refined this idea, distinguishing between **higher and lower pleasures**, emphasizing that intellectual and moral pleasures are superior to mere physical gratification.

There are two main branches:

- **Act Utilitarianism**: Assesses each individual action based on whether it produces the most utility.

- **Rule Utilitarianism**: Advocates following rules that generally lead to the greatest good, even if a specific case might suggest otherwise.

Example

Imagine a doctor with five patients, each in need of a different organ to survive. A healthy person walks into the hospital for a check-up. **Act utilitarianism** might, in theory, justify sacrificing the one to save the five, as it maximizes total lives saved. However, **rule utilitarianism** would reject this, recognizing that allowing doctors to kill patients would lead to societal mistrust and long-term harm—thus decreasing overall well-being.

Why It Works

Utilitarianism works because it provides a **clear, outcome-focused approach** to moral decision-making. It avoids rigid rules and adapts to circumstances, making it flexible in complex, real-world scenarios. It encourages impartiality—every person's happiness counts equally—and helps balance competing interests in a pluralistic society.

How It Works

The model involves:

1. **Identifying all potential actions**.

2. **Predicting outcomes** of each.

3. **Measuring consequences** in terms of happiness, well-being, or suffering.

4. **Choosing the action** that produces the most net benefit.

It relies on cost-benefit reasoning, often using data, forecasting, and stakeholder analysis.

Application

Utilitarianism is widely used in:

- **Public policy**: Evaluating laws by their social outcomes.

- **Healthcare**: Allocating scarce resources (e.g., triage in emergencies).

- **Business ethics**: Considering environmental or labour impacts.

- **AI ethics**: Programming machines to act in the best interest of the most people.

Key Insights

- Moral decisions should aim to **maximize well-being**.

- **Consequences** matter more than intentions.

- Equity and impartiality are central—every life counts.

- Short-term gains must be weighed against long-term impact.

- Ideal for **complex trade-offs** involving many stakeholders.

In essence, **Utilitarianism** offers a rational, outcome-based guide to ethical action—especially in a world where hard choices are often unavoidable.

73. Deontology

Deontology is a moral philosophy that judges the **morality of actions based on rules and duties**, rather than consequences. The term comes from the Greek *"deon"*, meaning duty. Most famously articulated by **Immanuel Kant** in the 18th century, deontology emphasizes that **some actions are morally right or wrong in themselves**, regardless of outcomes.

Theoretical Basis

Kantian deontology is grounded in the concept of the **categorical imperative**—a universal moral law that applies to all rational beings. One of Kant's key formulations is: **"Act only according to that maxim whereby you can at the same time will that it should become a universal law."** This means you should only act in ways you'd be okay with everyone else acting, universally.

Deontology holds that people must be treated as **ends in themselves**, never merely as means to an end. Moral worth lies in the **intention behind the action**, not its result.

Example

Consider lying to protect a friend from harm. A **utilitarian** might approve the lie if it leads to better outcomes. A **deontologist**, however, may argue that **lying is inherently wrong**, regardless of the consequence, because it violates a universal moral duty to be honest.

In another case, a doctor might refuse to euthanize a suffering patient, even if doing so would end their pain, because taking a life may violate the doctor's duty to preserve it.

Why It Works

Deontology works because it **upholds consistent moral standards**. It provides **moral clarity** in complex situations and protects individual rights by refusing to sacrifice one person's well-being for the sake of others. It offers a **principled framework** that avoids "ends justify the means" thinking, which can be ethically dangerous.

By focusing on rules, it helps maintain **trust, fairness, and justice** in both personal and societal relationships.

How It Works

Deontological reasoning involves:

1. Identifying the **moral duty or rule**.

2. Testing it against the idea of **universalizability**.

3. Assessing whether the action **respects others as autonomous beings**.

4. Acting from a sense of duty, not personal gain or emotion.

The core is not what happens, but whether you do what is **right**.

Application

Deontology is applied in:

- **Law and justice systems**: Upholding rights regardless of outcomes.

- **Medical ethics**: "Do no harm" as a non-negotiable duty.

- **Human rights**: Enforcing moral principles even when inconvenient.

- **Organizational ethics**: Following codes of conduct even under pressure.

Key Insights

- Some actions are **inherently right or wrong**, independent of outcomes.

- **Intentions and principles** matter more than results.

- Moral behaviour means acting from **duty**, not just preference.

- Rights and duties form the **ethical backbone** of fair societies.

- Deontology provides moral limits on utilitarian logic.

In essence, **Deontology** teaches that **doing the right thing matters—even when it's hard**, and that ethical integrity begins with moral duty.

74. Virtue Ethics

Virtue Ethics is a moral philosophy that emphasizes **character and virtues** rather than rules (as in deontology) or consequences (as in utilitarianism) as the foundation of ethical behaviour. Rooted in **Aristotle's** work in ancient Greece, Virtue Ethics asks not "What should I do?" but rather **"What kind of person should I be?"**

Theoretical Basis

Virtue Ethics is grounded in the idea that moral excellence is achieved through the cultivation of **habits** that develop virtuous character traits—such as **courage, honesty, temperance, justice, humility, and wisdom**. Aristotle called this state of moral maturity **"eudaimonia"**, often translated as **"flourishing"** or "the good life." It is not about momentary pleasure but about living in accordance with reason, purpose, and virtue.

Unlike deontology or consequentialism, Virtue Ethics doesn't provide strict formulas. It recognizes that moral life is complex and context-dependent. The goal is to exercise **practical wisdom** (*phronesis*)—the judgment to act rightly, in the right way, at the right time.

Example

Imagine someone finds a lost wallet full of cash.

- A **utilitarian** might decide to keep it if they believe more good will come from using the money.

- A **deontologist** may return it out of duty, regardless of circumstance.

- A **virtue ethicist** returns it because that's what an honest and just person would do—**not out of obligation, but because it reflects good character**.

Why It Works

Virtue Ethics works because it focuses on **long-term moral development**, not just isolated decisions. By cultivating good character, people are more likely to make wise, ethical choices across varied situations. It promotes **moral consistency**, emotional intelligence, and deep personal integrity, encouraging people to aspire to be their best selves rather than merely follow rules or maximize outcomes.

How It Works

Virtue is built through **habitual practice**:

1. Observe virtuous role models.

2. Reflect on values and internalize virtues.

3. Apply virtues in daily life.

4. Refine character through experience and reflection.

Over time, ethical behaviour becomes a **natural expression of character**, not a forced decision.

Application

Virtue Ethics is widely used in:

- **Leadership development**: Focusing on character, not just strategy.

- **Education**: Teaching values and moral reasoning.

- **Professional ethics**: Guiding behaviour in medicine, law, and counselling.

- **Personal growth**: Encouraging life-long moral development.

Key Insights

- Ethical behaviour stems from **who you are**, not just what you do.

- **Character is developed**, not fixed.

- **Role models** and habits shape moral identity.

- Virtue requires **balance**—courage without recklessness, honesty without cruelty.

- Ethical living is a **lifelong journey**, not a checklist.

In essence, **Virtue Ethics** reminds us that becoming good is the foundation for doing good—and that morality begins with character.

75. Social Contract

The Social Contract is a foundational concept in political philosophy that explains the **legitimacy of authority and governance** as arising from an **implicit agreement** between individuals and the state. Rather than viewing political power as divinely ordained or enforced by brute force, the Social Contract model posits that individuals **consent**, either explicitly or tacitly, to surrender some freedoms in exchange for **security, order, and collective benefit**.

Theoretical Basis

The Social Contract has roots in Enlightenment thinking and was shaped by philosophers such as **Thomas Hobbes, John Locke**, and **Jean-Jacques Rousseau**:

- **Hobbes** believed people in a state of nature would live in constant fear and conflict ("nasty, brutish, and short") and thus willingly submit to an absolute sovereign for peace.

- **Locke** argued for a contract to protect natural rights—**life, liberty, and property**—and justified rebellion if the state violates these rights.

- **Rousseau** emphasized that the general will, or collective good, should guide the contract, supporting more democratic ideals.

The underlying idea is that **societies function through mutual agreement**, not coercion, and that rights and duties are established through this social framework.

Example

A modern example is **taxation**. Citizens agree to pay taxes and obey laws in return for public goods like infrastructure, education, and protection by law enforcement. If a government uses tax money for corrupt purposes or suppresses rights, the contract is considered broken— justifying protest or reform.

In digital spaces, we see a new kind of social contract: users give up some privacy in exchange for access to free platforms like social media. The legitimacy of this exchange depends on transparency and trust.

Why It Works

The Social Contract works because it creates a **shared understanding** of the balance between freedom and responsibility. It legitimizes authority by rooting it in **consent rather than coercion** and helps form **cohesive societies** where rules are obeyed not out of fear, but out of agreement.

It also provides a **moral and legal foundation** for justice, rights, and civic engagement.

How It Works

It functions through:

1. **Implied agreement**: Individuals accept laws and norms.

2. **Institutional enforcement**: Governments uphold agreed-upon rules.

3. **Accountability**: Citizens have mechanisms (e.g. voting, protest) to challenge breaches.

This reciprocity ensures stability and adaptability in societies.

Application

- **Politics**: Foundations of democracy, constitutional law, and civil rights.

- **Business ethics**: Corporate social responsibility as a contract with society.

- **Digital ethics**: Debates over data privacy and platform accountability.

- **Education and work**: Shared codes of conduct and expectations.

Key Insights

- Authority requires **consent** to be legitimate.

- Rights come with **responsibilities**.

- Trust in systems depends on honouring the agreement.

- Breaches of the contract justify resistance or reform.

- The Social Contract evolves with societal values and norms.

In essence, the **Social Contract** reminds us that society is a **collaborative construction**, sustained by mutual agreement, trust, and shared responsibility.

76. Stoicism

Stoicism is a practical philosophy and mental model that teaches individuals to cultivate **inner resilience, rational thinking**, and **emotional discipline** by focusing on what they can control and accepting what they cannot. Originating in ancient Greece and developed further in Rome by thinkers like **Epictetus**, **Seneca**, and **Marcus Aurelius**, Stoicism offers a timeless framework for navigating life's challenges with clarity and composure.

Theoretical Basis

At its core, Stoicism separates reality into two categories:

1. **Things within our control**: Our thoughts, beliefs, judgments, actions, and attitudes.

2. **Things outside our control**: Other people's actions, outcomes, external events, and even our own health or reputation.

Stoics argue that **suffering arises not from events themselves**, but from our **interpretation and emotional response** to those events. By mastering our internal world, we can remain virtuous and undisturbed in the face of external chaos.

Virtue—defined as wisdom, courage, justice, and temperance—is the only true good in Stoicism. Success is measured not by wealth or fame, but by **living in accordance with reason and nature**.

Example

Imagine being passed over for a promotion. A Stoic response would be: "The decision was not within my control, but my reaction is. I will remain calm, reflect on my performance, and continue to act with integrity." Rather than being consumed by disappointment or resentment, the Stoic channels energy into self-improvement and acceptance.

Marcus Aurelius, a Roman emperor, practiced this daily amidst war and political intrigue—using Stoic journaling to reinforce inner strength and moral clarity.

Why It Works

Stoicism works because it shifts attention to the **only arena we truly influence**: our own mind. This helps reduce anxiety, frustration, and impulsive behaviour. In a chaotic or uncertain world, the ability to remain centred and act according to principle is incredibly powerful.

It encourages emotional **equanimity**, reduces unnecessary suffering, and builds mental toughness—qualities that enhance both personal well-being and leadership.

How It Works

Stoic practice includes:

- **Negative visualization**: Imagining loss to build gratitude.

- **Voluntary discomfort**: Training resilience through occasional hardship.

- **Reflection**: Daily journaling and self-examination.

- **Dichotomy of control**: Constantly distinguishing between controllables and uncontrollables.

These tools help cultivate a disciplined, proactive mindset.

Application

- **Leadership**: Making clear-headed decisions under pressure.

- **Mental health**: Reducing anxiety through perspective shifts.

- **Conflict resolution**: Responding calmly and rationally.

- **Athletics and performance**: Focusing on effort, not outcome.

Key Insights

- Peace comes from focusing only on what you can control.

- Virtue is the highest goal—not success or pleasure.

- Emotional mastery leads to freedom and clarity.

- Adversity is an opportunity for character development.

- Stoicism is not passive acceptance, but active resilience.

In essence, **Stoicism** offers a mindset for living with **grace under pressure**—anchoring action in wisdom, not impulse.

77. Existentialism

Existentialism is a philosophical and psychological framework that focuses on **individual freedom, choice, and responsibility** in an often **absurd or indifferent universe**. It asserts that meaning is not inherent in the world but must be **created by each person** through their actions, commitments, and personal values. This mental model has deep roots in the works of thinkers like **Søren Kierkegaard, Friedrich Nietzsche, Jean-Paul Sartre, Simone de Beauvoir**, and **Albert Camus**.

Theoretical Basis

Existentialism emerged as a response to the alienation of modern life, the decline of religious authority, and the trauma of world wars. It begins with the premise that **existence precedes essence**—in other words, we are not born with a predetermined purpose. Instead, we define ourselves through our choices.

A key idea is the **burden of freedom**: while we are radically free to choose how we live, that freedom comes with the responsibility of creating meaning in a meaningless world. Concepts like **authenticity, absurdity**, and **bad faith** (self-deception) are central to the existentialist mindset.

Example

Imagine a person stuck in a high-paying but unfulfilling job. An existentialist would say that continuing in that role without questioning its alignment with their values is an act of **bad faith**—living inauthentically. By acknowledging their freedom and accepting the anxiety that comes with it, they can choose to pursue a path that aligns with their deeper sense of purpose, even if it's riskier or unconventional.

Albert Camus illustrates existentialism through the myth of **Sisyphus**, eternally pushing a boulder uphill. Camus argues that even in the face of a futile task, we can find dignity and meaning by **choosing our attitude** toward it.

Why It Works

Existentialism works because it places meaning and agency back in the hands of the individual. In a world where external structures often feel inadequate or rigid, this model encourages **personal empowerment** and **moral accountability**. It recognizes the emotional complexity of being human—fear, anxiety, doubt—but offers a path through it.

How It Works

The model unfolds through:

1. **Radical self-awareness**.

2. **Confronting existential anxiety** honestly.

3. **Making authentic choices** based on personal values.

4. **Accepting consequences** without escape into ideology or excuses.

Existentialism invites people to live deliberately and fully.

Application

- **Psychotherapy**: Especially in existential and humanistic counselling.

- **Career and identity exploration**.

- **Art and literature**: As a lens to explore freedom and alienation.

- **Leadership**: Emphasizing purpose and responsibility.

Key Insights

- Life has no fixed meaning—you must create it.

- Freedom is real, but it comes with weight.

- Avoiding responsibility leads to inauthenticity.

- Embrace uncertainty—it's part of being human.

- Meaning is made through **choice, courage, and commitment**.

In essence, **Existentialism** challenges you to stop waiting for meaning—and start living it.

78. Golden Mean

The Golden Mean is a philosophical and ethical concept that promotes **moderation** as the key to virtue. Rooted in **Aristotelian ethics**, the Golden Mean proposes that **virtue lies between two extremes**—excess and deficiency. It is not about mediocrity, but about finding the **balanced and appropriate response** in any situation.

Theoretical Basis

Aristotle introduced the Golden Mean in his work *Nicomachean Ethics*. He argued that moral virtue is not innate, but developed through habit and rational judgment. Each virtue lies on a spectrum between two vices:

- **Courage** is the mean between **recklessness** (excess) and **cowardice** (deficiency).

- **Generosity** lies between **wastefulness** and **stinginess**.

- **Confidence** falls between **arrogance** and **insecurity**.

The Golden Mean is context-dependent. What is "moderate" for one person or situation may differ for another. The model calls for **practical wisdom (phronesis)**—the ability to discern the right action in varying circumstances.

Example

Imagine someone faced with criticism.

- Reacting with **rage** is excessive.

- Avoiding confrontation entirely is a deficiency.

- Responding with **calm assertiveness**, acknowledging the feedback while standing one's ground, reflects the Golden Mean.

Similarly, in leadership, micromanagement (excess control) and total hands-off detachment (deficiency) are both ineffective. A balanced leader practices **engaged delegation**, providing support without suffocating autonomy.

Why It Works

The Golden Mean works because it recognizes that human behaviour is rarely black-and-white. It provides a **flexible yet principled** framework for decision-making. Instead of rigid rules or unpredictable emotions, it encourages **balanced judgment**, which leads to more sustainable and ethical outcomes over time.

It also helps avoid the extremes that often cause dysfunction—overconfidence, overreaction, overindulgence—by anchoring actions in **reasoned moderation**.

How It Works

1. **Identify the virtue relevant to the situation** (e.g., honesty, courage, patience).

2. **Recognize the two extremes**—what too much or too little of that virtue looks like.

3. **Aim for the midpoint**, adjusting for context, personality, and impact.

4. **Practice habitually**, refining judgment over time.

The key is not rigid neutrality, but **active balance** informed by reflection and experience.

Application

- **Ethical decision-making** in leadership and business.

- **Personal development**: Cultivating character through balanced behaviour.

- **Conflict resolution**: Choosing response over reaction.

- **Parenting and education**: Modelling balanced conduct.

Key Insights

- Virtue is not fixed—it's dynamic and contextual.

- Extremes, even with good intent, often become vices.

- Balance requires awareness, discipline, and wisdom.

- The Golden Mean nurtures resilience, fairness, and moral clarity.

- Ethical excellence is built through **habitual moderation**.

In essence, the **Golden Mean** reminds us that wisdom often lies not in choosing sides, but in choosing balance.

79. Occasionalism

Occasionalism is a philosophical theory in metaphysics that proposes **God (or a divine agent) is the only true cause** of all events in the universe. According to this view, what we perceive as causal relationships between objects or events are not real causes but merely **"occasions"** for divine intervention. Developed primarily by **Islamic philosopher Al-Ghazali** and later by **Nicolas Malebranche**, Occasionalism challenges the assumption that physical objects or human wills have independent causal power.

Theoretical Basis

The core idea is that **created things cannot be true causes** because they lack the power to initiate or sustain action. For example, when fire burns paper, it's not the fire causing the paper to burn. Instead, the presence of fire is merely the **occasion** for God to bring about the burning. In this framework, **God alone sustains and orchestrates all events**, moment by moment.

Malebranche, a 17th-century French philosopher, applied this model to the mind-body problem. He argued that when the mind wills the body to move, God—not the will itself—is the actual cause of the physical movement.

Example

Imagine you flip a light switch and the light turns on. Most people assume the flipping caused the light to turn on via electricity. An occasionalist would argue that your flipping the switch merely **occurs alongside** the light turning on, and that **God causes** the light to illuminate on that occasion.

This idea parallels certain spiritual beliefs today, where outcomes are seen as divinely willed rather than mechanically caused.

Why It Works

While Occasionalism is metaphysical rather than empirical, it addresses gaps in human understanding of causation — especially in pre-modern contexts. It emphasizes **humility before the complexity of existence**, suggesting that what we assume to be cause and effect may be **illusionary or incomplete**.

It also served as a response to **sceptical critiques of causality**, such as those by David Hume, who later questioned the logical basis of causal inference.

How It Works

Occasionalism operates on the idea that:

1. Created beings have no autonomous causal power.

2. God continuously intervenes to maintain the order of the universe.

3. What we see as causation is **correlation with divine intention**.

This implies a **constant dependence** on a higher agency for all events.

Application

- **Theology**: Used in Islamic, Christian, and some mystical traditions to emphasize divine omnipotence.

- **Philosophy of mind**: In early attempts to resolve dualism (mind-body interaction).

- **Ethics and spirituality**: Reinforcing reliance on divine will over material causes.

Key Insights

- Causation may not be inherent—only perceived.

- Events might require metaphysical or divine explanation.

- Human agency and natural laws may be **instruments**, not sources.

- Encourages epistemic humility and spiritual reflection.

- Challenges assumptions about autonomy and control.

In essence, **Occasionalism** invites us to reconsider the nature of cause and effect—not as fixed mechanics, but as **expressions of a deeper, possibly divine, orchestration**.

80. Libertarianism

Libertarianism is a political and ethical philosophy centred on the value of **individual liberty**, emphasizing **personal autonomy, free markets, voluntary association, and minimal government intervention**. At its core, Libertarianism holds that people should be **free to live as they choose**, provided they **do not infringe on the rights of others**. It is grounded in the belief that freedom is not just a preference, but a moral necessity.

Theoretical Basis

The roots of Libertarianism lie in **classical liberalism**, with influences from Enlightenment thinkers like **John Locke**, who emphasized natural rights to life, liberty, and property. In modern times, it has been championed by philosophers like **Robert Nozick** and economists such as **Friedrich Hayek** and **Milton Friedman**.

Nozick's book *Anarchy, State, and Utopia* argues that a "minimal state" limited to protecting individuals from force, theft, and fraud is the only morally justifiable form of governance. Anything more—like redistributive welfare— violates individual rights.

Example

Consider taxation. A libertarian might argue that compulsory taxation for social programs constitutes a violation of individual property rights. If person A earns income through voluntary exchange, taking part of it to support person B—without consent—amounts to coercion. Instead, libertarians support **voluntary charity** and private solutions to social issues.

In business, a libertarian approach favors **deregulation**, allowing markets to operate freely under the belief that competition and innovation best serve public needs.

Why It Works

Libertarianism works when **personal responsibility, voluntary cooperation, and decentralized decision-making** are valued. It reduces bureaucracy, increases efficiency, and encourages innovation. By limiting centralized power, it protects against government overreach and respects diverse values in pluralistic societies.

It appeals strongly in areas where **freedom and autonomy are threatened** or where **market-based solutions outperform state intervention**.

How It Works

The model operates on key principles:

1. **Non-aggression principle**: Individuals should not initiate force against others.

2. **Self-ownership**: Each person owns their body, labour, and the fruits of their labour.

3. **Voluntary exchange**: All interactions should be consensual.

4. **Rule of law**: A minimal state ensures protection of rights, contracts, and property.

It's a **bottom-up** model of order and value creation.

Application

- **Policy**: Advocating for free trade, low taxes, school choice, and civil liberties.

- **Technology**: Embraced in crypto and decentralized tech communities.

- **Lifestyle**: Emphasizing self-reliance, minimalism, and personal freedom.

- **Economics**: Supporting entrepreneurship and deregulation.

Key Insights

- Freedom is the foundation of ethical and prosperous societies.

- Centralized power often leads to coercion and inefficiency.

- Consent and voluntary exchange are moral imperatives.

- Individual responsibility is crucial for social cohesion.

- Markets and liberty tend to be mutually reinforcing.

In essence, **Libertarianism** offers a mental model of human flourishing through **freedom, choice, and minimal constraint**—trusting people to govern themselves.

Strategic Thinking and Problem-Solving Models:

81. Strategy vs. Tactics

The **Strategy vs. Tactics** mental model distinguishes between the **big-picture direction** (strategy) and the **specific actions** (tactics) taken to achieve that direction. Understanding the difference—and how they interrelate—is essential for effective decision-making, leadership, and long-term success.

Theoretical Basis

This model originates in **military theory**, with thinkers like **Sun Tzu**, **Carl von Clausewitz**, and later, modern business strategists distinguishing between these two levels of action. Strategy is about **choosing the right battles**; tactics are about **winning those battles**. Strategy answers *"What are we trying to achieve and why?"*, while tactics answer *"How will we achieve it?"*

In short:

- **Strategy = Long-term vision + overarching plan**

- **Tactics = Short-term actions + tools used to execute the strategy**

Example

In a business context, a company's **strategy** might be to become the market leader in eco-friendly packaging within five years. Its **tactics** might include influencer marketing campaigns, a pricing discount for first-time users, partnerships with sustainable suppliers, and launching a line of biodegradable containers.

If the company runs aggressive ads (a tactic) without aligning them to its sustainability mission (its strategy), it may win short-term attention but lose long-term trust.

Why It Works

This model works because it helps prevent **misalignment** between daily actions and long-term goals. Without strategy, tactics can become **busywork**—activity without direction. Without tactics, strategy becomes **abstract or wishful thinking**. Strategic clarity ensures that energy is spent where it moves the needle, while tactical skill ensures execution is effective and responsive.

It also helps with **prioritization**. Knowing what serves the strategy allows you to focus on **high-leverage actions**.

How It Works

1. **Define the objective**: What's the end goal?

2. **Craft the strategy**: What's the best route to get there?

3. **Select tactics**: What specific actions will move us forward?

4. **Ensure alignment**: Regularly check if tactics are serving the strategy.

5. **Adjust dynamically**: If tactics aren't working, change them—but the strategy may still hold.

Application

- **Business**: Product launches, marketing plans, customer acquisition.

- **Military & security**: Campaign-level decisions vs. field manoeuvres.

- **Politics**: Broad policy goals vs. day-to-day messaging.

- **Personal development**: Career goals vs. daily habits or learning tasks.

Key Insights

- Strategy sets **direction**; tactics drive **motion**.

- Tactical success is meaningless without strategic alignment.

- A great strategy with poor tactics fails—so does the reverse.

- Tactical decisions must **serve strategic purpose**, not just urgency.

- Strategy evolves slowly; tactics evolve quickly.

In essence, **Strategy vs. Tactics** is about thinking both **long-term and short-term simultaneously,** ensuring that what you do today truly serves where you want to go tomorrow.

82. OODA Loop

The **OODA Loop**—short for **Observe, Orient, Decide, Act**—is a decision-making framework developed by U.S. Air Force Colonel **John Boyd**. Originally designed to give fighter pilots a strategic edge in combat, the model has since been widely adopted in business, leadership, cybersecurity, and high-stakes decision-making environments. The core idea is that **speed and adaptability in decision-making** can provide a crucial advantage, especially in rapidly changing or competitive environments.

Theoretical Basis

The OODA Loop is grounded in **military strategy**, **systems thinking**, and **cognitive psychology**. Boyd argued that the key to winning in complex, high-speed conflicts isn't brute strength—it's the ability to **process information and adapt faster than your opponent**. The loop is iterative and continuous, allowing for flexible responses as situations evolve.

The four stages are:

1. **Observe** – Gather data from your environment (internal and external).

2. **Orient** – Analyse the data in context, considering biases, experience, and situational awareness.

3. **Decide** – Choose a course of action based on your orientation.

4. **Act** – Execute the decision swiftly, then re-enter the loop with new information.

Example

In business, consider a company facing a sudden market disruption—like a competitor launching a revolutionary product. A company using the OODA Loop would:

- **Observe**: Monitor customer reactions, competitor moves, and internal performance.

- **Orient**: Analyse how this impacts their value proposition, using market insights and internal strengths.

- **Decide**: Develop a counter-strategy—maybe a product upgrade or marketing pivot.

- **Act**: Implement the change decisively, and return to observation to adjust further if needed.

Companies like Amazon, SpaceX, and certain military units excel by cycling through the loop **faster and more accurately** than competitors, maintaining strategic agility.

Why It Works

The OODA Loop works because it emphasizes **continuous learning and iteration**, enabling faster adaptation. In environments where conditions evolve rapidly, static strategies fail. By staying dynamic and responsive, you

disrupt your opponent's decision-making, causing delays, confusion, or collapse of their strategy.

It's not just speed—it's **clarity, feedback, and momentum**.

How It Works

- Break problems into short decision cycles.

- Stay aware of changing conditions.

- Adapt your orientation with new input (be aware of biases).

- Make decisions quickly, but revise them if needed.

- Act with conviction to stay ahead.

Application

- **Military and law enforcement**: Tactical operations and threat response.

- **Startups**: Rapid product development and market fit adjustments.

- **Leadership**: Crisis management and decision agility.

- **Negotiation and strategy**: Staying unpredictable and proactive.

Key Insights

- Speed and adaptability beat size and planning alone.

- Situational awareness is critical—**orientation shapes everything.**

- Fast, iterative decisions **disrupt competitors' tempo.**

- Continuous loops enable resilience in dynamic environments.

- The faster and more accurately you cycle, the more control you gain.

In essence, the **OODA Loop** helps you out-think and outmanoeuvre complexity—not through force, but through **strategic agility.**

83. Sunken Ship Fallacy

The Sunken Ship Fallacy is a mental model that warns against continuing with a failing endeavour simply because **you've already invested heavily** in it—whether that investment is time, money, energy, or emotion. It is closely related to the **sunk cost fallacy**, but with a stronger emphasis on **emotional attachment and identity entanglement**—often felt when letting go feels like abandoning "your ship."

This model encourages you to ask: *"If I hadn't already put so much into this, would I still choose to stay?"*

Theoretical Basis

The fallacy stems from **cognitive dissonance**, **loss aversion**, and **commitment bias**. People find it difficult to admit past decisions were wrong or unproductive, and they fear "wasting" what's already gone. Ironically, by trying to avoid waste, they often throw **good resources after bad**, digging deeper into failure.

The metaphor of a **sunken ship** implies that the vessel (project, relationship, career path) is already lost—continuing to bail out water or rebuild what has fundamentally failed only ensures further loss.

Example

Imagine an entrepreneur who has poured five years and thousands of dollars into a failing business. Revenue is flat, the market has moved on, and new competitors dominate. Instead of pivoting or exiting, they double down—investing more money and time in the hope that things will turn around. The longer they stay, the harder it becomes to leave, not because the future looks brighter, but because the **past is weighing too heavily**.

Similarly, someone might stay in a toxic relationship or unfulfilling career just because they've already "put in so much." The emotional and psychological commitment becomes a trap.

Why It Works

Recognizing the Sunken Ship Fallacy works because it **frees decision-making from the chains of the past**. It allows you to **cut losses early**, focus on future value, and invest resources in new opportunities rather than trying to recover irrecoverable investments.

It shifts attention from **past cost to future potential**, which is the only rational basis for action.

How It Works

1. Acknowledge what's been lost—financially, emotionally, or socially.

2. Ask yourself: *Would I start this today, knowing what I know now?*

3. Focus on opportunity cost—what staying prevents you from doing.

4. Make future-focused decisions, even if emotionally difficult.

Application

- **Business**: Abandoning unprofitable projects or markets.

- **Personal life**: Leaving harmful habits, relationships, or sunk ambitions.

- **Investing**: Exiting positions based on future outlook, not entry cost.

- **Time management**: Stopping books, courses, or efforts that no longer serve you.

Key Insights

- Sunk costs are gone—**don't let them dictate your future**.

- Letting go is not failure—it's strategic clarity.

- Emotional investment can cloud logic.

- Wise decisions prioritize **where you're going**, not where you've been.

- Staying on a sunken ship only guarantees you go down with it.

In essence, the **Sunken Ship Fallacy** reminds us that survival—and success—often depends on knowing **when to abandon what can't be saved**.

84. First Mover Advantage

First Mover Advantage is a strategic mental model that refers to the **competitive edge gained by being the first to enter a market or create a new category**. The idea is that by arriving early, a company can **establish brand recognition, secure key resources**, build **customer loyalty**, and **set industry standards** before competitors catch up.

Theoretical Basis

The concept comes from **strategic management and game theory**, where timing and positioning can determine long-term dominance. Being first allows a company to **shape consumer preferences**, lock in suppliers and distributors, and benefit from **learning curves** and **network effects**—advantages that make it difficult for latecomers to compete.

However, this strategy is not without risk. The model is only effective when early entrants can **sustain their lead** through innovation, scalability, or protective moats (e.g. patents, data, switching costs).

Example

A classic example is **Amazon** in online retail. While not the first e-commerce site, it was the first to scale efficiently, dominate logistics, and build massive infrastructure—turning its early position into a self-reinforcing ecosystem. Another is **Coca-Cola**, which established itself early in the soft drink category and built an iconic brand that continues to hold market leadership more than a century later.

On the tech front, **Google** wasn't the first search engine, but it was the first to perfect the PageRank algorithm and create a monetizable model through AdWords—securing a dominant foothold.

Why It Works

First Mover Advantage works because early entrants can **build brand equity**, gather **customer data**, refine their offerings through **trial and error**, and create **switching costs** that discourage users from jumping ship. They can also create **path dependency**, where the structure of the market starts to rely on their ecosystem, tools, or formats.

When successful, this leads to **self-reinforcing dominance**.

How It Works

1. Identify or create a new market/category.

2. Launch with sufficient scale, speed, and visibility.

3. Lock in early adopters and build brand loyalty.

4. Use the lead time to refine operations and expand reach.

5. Reinforce position with IP, partnerships, or superior user experience.

Speed must be paired with **sustainability**—being first isn't enough if execution fails.

Application

- **Tech startups**: Launching new platforms or products ahead of competitors.

- **Pharmaceuticals**: Securing patents for breakthrough drugs.

- **Media and content**: Establishing thought leadership in emerging niches.

- **Consumer goods**: Capturing shelf space and customer habits early.

Key Insights

- First to market can mean first to dominate—**if the advantage is maintained**.

- Success depends on **speed, scale, and follow-through**.

- Early leads can generate **network effects and brand loyalty**.

- It's risky—**pioneers may fail**, while settlers thrive.

- Requires **vision, resources, and staying power**.

In essence, **First Mover Advantage** is about **owning the ground before the race begins**—but knowing how to **defend it once others arrive**.

85. Fast Follower Strategy

Fast Follower Strategy is a business and innovation mental model that focuses on **quickly adopting and improving upon successful innovations pioneered by others**, rather than being the first to market. The core idea is to **avoid the high risk and cost of early innovation** while still capturing significant market share by entering soon after the trailblazer—with a better, cheaper, or more refined offering.

Theoretical Basis

This strategy stems from competitive strategy theory and innovation diffusion models. While **first movers** may enjoy early market attention and temporary monopoly power, they often face **high R&D costs**, **uncertain demand**, and **unrefined products**. Fast followers, in contrast, let the market validate the idea, learn from the pioneer's mistakes, and **move in with improved timing, execution, or efficiency**.

This model works best in dynamic industries where **learning speed**, **agility**, and **customer responsiveness** outweigh the advantage of being first.

Example

Consider **Facebook**. While it was not the first social network (MySpace and Friendster came earlier), it observed what worked and what failed. Facebook rapidly improved the user experience, scaled infrastructure, and focused on real identities, becoming the dominant platform. Similarly, **Samsung** built its smartphone empire by following Apple's iPhone launch closely—adapting features and responding swiftly to market feedback.

In both cases, fast followers reaped long-term benefits while avoiding many of the **pioneer pitfalls**.

Why It Works

Fast Follower Strategy works because **innovation is expensive and risky**, but **imitation plus execution is often more profitable**. Followers don't need to guess what the market wants—they watch, adapt, and deploy with precision. This approach also allows companies to capitalize on **technological readiness, market awareness, and improved timing**.

It also capitalizes on **second-mover advantage**—the ability to optimize where others experimented.

How It Works

1. **Monitor industry trends and first movers.**

2. **Analyse market reception** and pinpoint flaws or gaps.

3. **Act quickly to adapt**, refine, and deliver a superior or more efficient alternative.

4. Leverage **stronger distribution, branding, or cost structures**.

5. Continue to **iterate and evolve** based on early insights and customer data.

Success relies on **speed, flexibility, and execution—not invention**.

Application

- **Startups**: Launching refined versions of emerging tech ideas.

- **Retail**: Imitating successful formats and improving operations.

- **Software**: Cloning features from market leaders and making them more accessible.

- **Global expansion**: Entering markets after a successful local pioneer.

Key Insights

- Being first isn't always best—**being better and faster can win**.

- Watch, learn, adapt: **agility beats originality in some markets**.

- Fast following requires **execution excellence**, not just imitation.

- The strategy reduces risk but still demands strategic boldness.

- Timing is everything—**too slow and you're forgotten, too early and you're punished**.

In essence, the **Fast Follower Strategy** thrives on **smart timing, adaptive thinking, and operational mastery**—not novelty alone.

86. Strategic Depth

Strategic Depth is a mental model drawn from **military strategy**, **business planning**, and **systems thinking** that refers to the **buffering, flexibility, and layers of support** that allow an individual, organization, or nation to absorb shocks and sustain operations over time. It emphasizes the importance of having **reserves, alternatives, and contingency plans**—not just in space (like territory), but in capacity, resources, and options.

Theoretical Basis

In military terms, strategic depth refers to the **geographical distance** between frontlines and critical assets, like capitals or supply chains. Nations with more depth can retreat, regroup, and counterattack. But the concept has evolved beyond geography: in modern strategy, it means having **layers of redundancy and resilience**—the ability to respond flexibly under pressure.

Strategic depth is also connected to **optionality, anti-fragility**, and **second-order thinking**. It means you're not relying on a single outcome or plan but have the capacity to adapt as conditions change.

Example

Consider a company that relies entirely on a single supplier. If that supplier fails, operations halt. Now imagine a company with strategic depth: multiple suppliers, backup inventory, diversified revenue streams, and a strong talent bench. When disruption strikes, it can pivot, endure, and recover faster.

In personal terms, a professional with strategic depth might have a main career, a secondary skill set, a financial buffer, and strong relationships. They are less vulnerable to unexpected career shifts or market downturns.

Why It Works

Strategic Depth works because **complex systems are vulnerable to single points of failure**. Whether it's a supply chain, political alliance, or personal plan, having layers of capacity enables survival, adaptation, and even growth under stress.

It transforms fragility into resilience and short-term wins into **sustainable success**.

How It Works

1. **Map your critical assets**—people, processes, partners.

2. Identify **vulnerabilities** and where you're overly reliant.

3. Build **redundancy**: backups, alternatives, flexible systems.

4. Strengthen **feedback loops** to detect issues early.

5. Create **buffer zones**—whether spatial, temporal, or financial.

Strategic depth is about preparation, not reaction.

Application

- **National defence**: Buffer zones, logistics networks, reserve forces.

- **Business strategy**: Supply chain diversification, R&D pipelines, multiple revenue sources.

- **Career development**: Learning new skills, building networks, having options.

- **Crisis management**: Layered responses, information flows, decision rights.

Key Insights

- Depth creates **resilience** under pressure.

- One-layer strategies are fragile, even if effective short-term.

- Strategic depth requires **investment upfront**—but pays off in stability.

- Flexibility is as important as strength.

- Winning long-term means thinking in **layers, not lines**.

In essence, **Strategic Depth** ensures you're not one bad move away from collapse—it gives you room to **manoeuvre, adapt, and endure.**

87. Kill Criteria

Kill Criteria is a decision-making mental model that helps individuals and organizations determine **when to stop, pivot, or abandon a project, strategy, or commitment**. It involves setting **predefined thresholds or conditions**—"kill points"—that, when met, **trigger an objective exit**, regardless of emotional attachment, sunk costs, or hopeful bias.

Theoretical Basis

This model is rooted in **behavioural economics** and **decision theory**, specifically addressing cognitive biases like the **sunk cost fallacy, optimism bias**, and **loss aversion**. Humans tend to stick with failing endeavours because of the time, money, or effort already invested. Kill Criteria counters this by creating **rational benchmarks** that guide action before emotion can cloud judgment.

It's often used in **startups, military strategy**, and **scientific experiments**, where resources are limited and failure must be recognized early to avoid catastrophic waste.

Example

A tech startup is testing a new product. Instead of charging blindly ahead, they set kill criteria: *"If we don't reach 10,000 users by month six or convert at least 5% of our beta testers to paying users, we will shut down the project."* When month six arrives and both metrics are unmet, they exit—even if emotionally invested—freeing resources for better opportunities.

This structured approach contrasts with "hope-driven" management, which often leads to overextension and failure to pivot in time.

Why It Works

Kill Criteria works because it **pre-commits you to rational action** before emotional bias takes hold. It reduces the risk of persisting in bad decisions and **creates clarity in ambiguity**. It also fosters a **learning-oriented culture**, where stopping is seen as strategic, not shameful.

By defining success and failure upfront, teams can act **decisively**, rather than dragging on in uncertainty.

How It Works

1. **Set clear goals** and identify measurable indicators of success.

2. Define **thresholds or conditions** that would justify discontinuation.

3. Commit in advance to honouring these kill points.

4. Regularly **review progress** against those metrics.

5. Take action—pivot, pause, or kill—when criteria are met.

This requires discipline, transparency, and a willingness to walk away from sunk investments.

Application

- **Startups**: Avoiding wasted funding on unscalable products.

- **Project management**: Stopping underperforming initiatives early.

- **Investing**: Selling assets based on pre-set loss limits.

- **Personal goals**: Knowing when to leave draining jobs or habits.

Key Insights

- Predefined exit rules protect against emotional traps.

- Not all persistence is wise—**strategic quitting is strength**.

- Objective measurement beats gut feeling in complex decisions.

- Kill Criteria enhances **agility, focus, and resource allocation**.

- It turns failure into learning, not loss.

In essence, the **Kill Criteria** model helps ensure that energy and resources are invested where they can truly make an impact—**and withdrawn where they can't**.

88. War of Attrition

The **War of Attrition** is a strategic mental model rooted in **game theory**, **evolutionary biology**, and **military history**. It describes a conflict where victory is achieved not through decisive action, but through **endurance**—outlasting the opponent by **absorbing costs longer** than they can. Rather than swift confrontation, this model is about **grinding resistance down over time** until the opposing side yields due to depleted resources, willpower, or patience.

Theoretical Basis

Originally developed in game theory and refined in **evolutionary strategies** (by biologists like John Maynard Smith), the War of Attrition is used to model contests where direct confrontation is too costly, and the outcome depends on **which player gives up first**. Each participant weighs the **benefit of winning** against the **accumulating cost of staying in the fight**.

In economics and politics, it's used to describe pricing wars, labour strikes, or legislative standoffs—any scenario where time, pressure, and cost are the primary weapons.

Example

Consider two rival companies engaged in a price war. Company A lowers its prices aggressively, hoping to outlast Company B, even at the expense of short-term profits. Company B does the same. Over time, both burn resources, but Company A, with deeper reserves or a stronger stomach for loss, eventually forces Company B to withdraw, capturing market share.

In nature, two animals may compete over a mate by displaying strength, not through direct combat, but by posturing. The longer each endures, the more energy they expend—until one gives up, and the other wins by **outlasting, not overpowering**.

Why It Works

The War of Attrition works because **many opponents don't lose—they quit**. It exploits the psychological and material costs of sustained pressure. If one party can tolerate the burden longer than the other, victory becomes a matter of endurance, not superiority.

This model also exposes hidden weaknesses—like poor planning, resource limits, or fragile motivation—that wouldn't appear in a short-term contest.

How It Works

1. Both sides enter conflict expecting eventual gain.

2. Costs accumulate the longer the conflict drags on.

3. No decisive victory occurs—just escalating pressure.

4. Eventually, the less committed or less resourced party yields.

Application

- **Business**: Pricing wars, endurance marketing, legal battles.

- **Politics**: Budget impasses, trade disputes, protest movements.

- **Personal goals**: Competitive sports, negotiation standoffs, personal willpower challenges.

Key Insights

- Winning doesn't always require speed—sometimes it requires **stamina**.

- Many "losses" are actually **forfeits** due to unsustainable cost.

- Emotional resilience and resource management are key.

- Outlasting can be as effective as outsmarting or overpowering.

- Know **your limits**—and your opponent's—before engaging.

In essence, the **War of Attrition** reminds us that in prolonged struggles, **victory often belongs to the last one standing**.

89. Chessboard Thinking

Chessboard Thinking is a strategic mental model that draws from the game of chess to illustrate how to approach **complex, multi-move decision-making**. It emphasizes **long-term planning, anticipating consequences**, and viewing problems in terms of **interrelated parts**—like a player reading not just the current move, but the entire board.

Theoretical Basis

This model is grounded in **game theory**, **systems thinking**, and **strategic foresight**. In chess, no piece moves in isolation; every decision affects the positioning of other pieces. Similarly, in life, business, or politics, outcomes are rarely the result of a single action but are shaped by a **series of interconnected decisions** made over time.

Chessboard Thinking helps one shift from **reactive choices** to **deliberate strategies**, balancing both **tactics (short-term manoeuvres)** and **strategy (long-term positioning)**.

Example

Consider a company launching a new product. A tactical thinker might focus on the immediate launch and short-term sales. A Chessboard Thinker, however, anticipates how competitors might react, how pricing affects future margins, how market perception could evolve, and how the launch fits into a five-year brand strategy. Each "move" is weighed in terms of its ripple effects.

In global politics, Chessboard Thinking can be seen in diplomacy or military planning, where leaders must anticipate opponents' moves and adapt strategies dynamically—just like in a chess game.

Why It Works

Chessboard Thinking works because **most real-world systems are dynamic**, with players, rules, and consequences constantly shifting. It prepares the mind to expect **countermoves, trade-offs, and unintended consequences**, fostering better judgment and adaptability. It also reduces impulsivity, forcing decisions to be weighed against future outcomes.

It promotes **second- and third-order thinking**, which is key to avoiding short-sighted errors.

How It Works

1. **Assess the board**: Understand the landscape—who the players are, what the resources and constraints are.

2. **Think ahead**: Visualize several moves forward— what might happen next, and after that?

3. **Anticipate reactions**: How will others respond to your actions?

4. **Balance tactics and strategy**: Make moves that serve both immediate and long-term goals.

5. **Adapt dynamically**: Be willing to revise plans as new information emerges.

Application

- **Leadership and business strategy**: Long-term planning and competitive analysis.

- **Negotiations**: Predicting the other party's response and planning accordingly.

- **Career development**: Aligning daily actions with long-term ambitions.

- **Crisis management**: Thinking several steps ahead in uncertain environments.

Key Insights

- Every move changes the game.

- Strategic patience beats short-term gain.

- Anticipation and foresight are learned skills.

- Success lies in **seeing the whole board**, not just one piece.

- Complex problems require **multi-move thinking**, not isolated reactions.

In essence, **Chessboard Thinking** teaches us to pause, plan, and play not just the next move—but the whole game.

90. Decoy Effect

The Decoy Effect, also known as **asymmetric dominance**, is a cognitive bias in decision-making where people's preferences between two options change when a third, **inferior but strategically designed option** is introduced. The decoy is not intended to be chosen; rather, its purpose is to make one of the original options appear more attractive by comparison.

Theoretical Basis

The Decoy Effect stems from **behavioural economics** and was first formally studied by researchers like **Dan Ariely**. It challenges the classical economic assumption that people make rational, consistent choices. Instead, it demonstrates that **context and comparison** play a powerful role in shaping preferences—even when the third option is irrelevant on its own.

This mental model is closely related to **choice architecture**, which shows that the way options are framed or structured can heavily influence decisions.

Example

Imagine you're choosing a subscription plan:

- **Option A**: Online access only — $59
- **Option B**: Print and online — $125

- **Option C (Decoy)**: Print only — $125

Most people initially prefer the cheaper online-only plan. But when Option C is introduced, suddenly Option B seems like a **much better deal**—more value for the same price. Although almost no one chooses Option C, its presence **nudges** people toward Option B. That's the Decoy Effect in action.

Why It Works

The Decoy Effect works because humans often struggle with **absolute evaluation** and rely instead on **relative comparison**. The decoy makes the target option appear superior in contrast, simplifying the decision-making process. It triggers **heuristic thinking**, where the brain seeks shortcuts to avoid cognitive overload.

It also plays on **loss aversion**—people perceive the decoy as offering less for the same price and are drawn to the "smarter" option.

How It Works

1. Start with two genuine options: A and B.

2. Introduce a third option (C) that is **clearly worse** than one (B) but **comparable**.

3. C makes B look like a better deal in **relative terms**.

4. This subtly **steers decisions** without changing the original offerings.

It doesn't manipulate directly—it leverages **perception**.

Application

- **Marketing and pricing strategies**: Subscription models, product tiers, menu pricing.

- **Policy design**: Nudging behaviour toward desired choices.

- **Negotiations**: Presenting unattractive alternatives to guide preference.

- **UX design**: Influencing user behaviour through feature comparisons.

Key Insights

- Choices are **context-dependent**, not purely rational.

- People evaluate **comparatively**, not in isolation.

- You can **influence preference without altering actual value**.

- The decoy must be **strategically inferior**, not obviously manipulative.

- Understanding the Decoy Effect helps avoid being subtly steered—and use it ethically.

In essence, the **Decoy Effect** reveals how subtle design can **reshape decisions**, not by changing the options—but by changing **how we see them**.

Psychological Resilience Models:

91. Post-Traumatic Growth

Post-Traumatic Growth (PTG) is a psychological model that describes the **positive psychological transformation** that can occur after experiencing **significant trauma or adversity**. Rather than focusing solely on the damage caused by trauma (as in PTSD), PTG emphasizes the **potential for growth, meaning, and renewed life purpose** that may emerge in its aftermath.

Theoretical Basis

Developed by psychologists **Richard Tedeschi** and **Lawrence Calhoun**, PTG is rooted in **positive psychology** and **existential psychology**. It proposes that while trauma can shake or even shatter an individual's core beliefs, this disruption also creates space for **rebuilding a new worldview**—often one that is more resilient, spiritually enriched, and appreciative of life.

PTG doesn't suggest that trauma is desirable or that suffering is a prerequisite for growth, but it acknowledges that **growth is possible as a response to suffering**.

Example

Consider someone who survives a life-threatening illness. While the experience may involve fear, pain, and loss, many survivors report profound changes afterward: a deeper appreciation for life, closer relationships, a shift in priorities, or a desire to contribute to others' well-being. They emerge not unchanged, but **transformed**.

This phenomenon is common among trauma survivors, including war veterans, bereaved individuals, and survivors of abuse or natural disasters.

Why It Works

PTG works because **crisis disrupts assumptions**, forcing individuals to confront questions of identity, mortality, and meaning. When supported appropriately, this process can lead to a **reconstruction of the self** on more solid, conscious, and purposeful foundations. Instead of returning to "normal," individuals construct a **new normal** that reflects their values and deeper insights.

This growth is often linked with increased **resilience**, **gratitude**, **empathy**, and **spiritual or existential depth**.

How It Works

1. **Trauma challenges core beliefs**.

2. Emotional distress creates **cognitive dissonance**.

3. The individual **reflects, questions, and re-evaluates** their worldview.

4. With support (therapy, social connection, meaning-making), the individual constructs a new narrative.

5. **Growth emerges**, often in five domains: personal strength, appreciation of life, new possibilities, spiritual development, and improved relationships.

Application

- **Therapy and counselling**: Helping clients reframe trauma and identify growth.

- **Healthcare**: Supporting recovery from chronic illness or injury.

- **Leadership**: Guiding teams through organizational crises.

- **Education**: Teaching students resilience and narrative reconstruction.

Key Insights

- Growth can coexist with pain—**one doesn't erase the other**.

- Trauma may dismantle—but also **rebuild**—identity and values.

- PTG is **not guaranteed**; it requires time, reflection, and support.

- Sharing stories and finding meaning accelerates healing.

- People can emerge from hardship **stronger, wiser, and more compassionate**.

In essence, **Post-Traumatic Growth** reminds us that even in the darkest seasons of life, there exists the potential for profound transformation.

92. Self-Distancing

Self-Distancing is a cognitive and emotional regulation strategy that involves **stepping back from one's immediate thoughts, feelings, or experiences** in order to gain clarity, reduce reactivity, and make more objective decisions. It's the practice of observing yourself as if from a third-person perspective—**like watching your thoughts as an outsider**, rather than being entangled in them.

Theoretical Basis

This model is grounded in research from **psychology and neuroscience**, particularly the work of **Ethan Kross** and others in the field of self-regulation. It draws from **cognitive behavioural therapy (CBT)**, **mindfulness**, and **Stoic philosophy**, all of which emphasize the value of perspective in managing emotions.

Self-distancing doesn't mean suppression or avoidance. Rather, it involves **acknowledging emotions without identifying with them**, creating space for more thoughtful and less reactive responses.

Example

Imagine you've received harsh criticism at work. The immediate response might be anger, shame, or defensiveness. A self-immersed reaction might sound like: *"I'm a failure."* In contrast, a self-distanced response reframes the experience: *"Why did Alex react that way to my presentation? What might I learn from this?"* By viewing the situation through a third-person lens—"What advice would I give a friend in this situation?"—you regulate your emotions more effectively.

This strategy is also seen in journaling or speaking about oneself using **your own name** instead of "I"—a technique shown to reduce anxiety and rumination.

Why It Works

Self-distancing works because it **breaks the cycle of emotional reactivity and rumination**. By creating psychological space, individuals can evaluate situations more rationally and act with intention rather than impulse. It helps separate the **self from the emotion**, allowing for **reflection without being overwhelmed**.

It also shifts brain activity from emotional centres (like the amygdala) toward regions involved in **reasoning and self-control**, supporting wiser decision-making.

How It Works

1. **Pause** and observe your thoughts without judgment.

2. **Reframe in third person**: "What is [your name] feeling right now?"

3. **Zoom out**: View the situation from a future or outsider perspective.

4. **Ask reflective questions**: "What would a calm version of me do?"

5. **Act with intention**, not from emotional impulse.

Practice strengthens this skill over time.

Application

- **Leadership**: Making clear-headed decisions in conflict.

- **Mental health**: Managing anxiety, anger, or self-doubt.

- **Education**: Helping students navigate emotional challenges.

- **Relationships**: De-escalating personal arguments.

Key Insights

- You are **not your thoughts**—you observe them.

- Distance creates **clarity, not coldness**.

- Perspective-taking improves **self-regulation**.

- Responding is stronger than reacting.

- Self-distancing supports **emotional intelligence and resilience**.

In essence, **Self-Distancing** is the art of creating space between **stimulus and response**, allowing wisdom to enter where instinct once ruled.

93. The Serenity Prayer Model

The Serenity Prayer Model is a mental framework derived from the famous prayer often attributed to **Reinhold Niebuhr**, which reads:

"God, grant me the serenity to accept the things I cannot change,
courage to change the things I can,
and wisdom to know the difference."

This model offers a powerful, practical lens for navigating **stress, uncertainty, and decision-making**. It encourages individuals to distinguish between **what is within their control** and **what is not**, and to act wisely and deliberately based on that distinction.

Theoretical Basis

The Serenity Prayer Model draws from principles in **Stoic philosophy**, **cognitive behavioural therapy (CBT)**, and **mindfulness practices**. In particular, it mirrors the Stoic dichotomy of control (Epictetus) and aligns with psychological concepts like **locus of control** and **acceptance-based coping**.

At its core, this model encourages:

1. **Acceptance** of the uncontrollable,

2. **Agency** in areas of influence, and

3. **Discernment** between the two.

Example

Consider someone facing a layoff due to company-wide restructuring. They cannot prevent the decision (beyond their control), but they can control how they respond— updating their resume, networking, managing stress, and maintaining a positive outlook. The serenity prayer model would guide them to **let go of frustration over the layoff itself** and focus energy on what they **can actively improve**.

Trying to control everything would lead to anxiety. Resignation to helplessness would breed passivity. The balance is key.

Why It Works

This model works because it helps **reduce wasted emotional energy** on things we cannot influence while empowering action where it matters. It cultivates a sense of **peace and purpose**, enhancing resilience and mental clarity. By practicing discernment, individuals can avoid both **burnout from overcontrol** and **learned helplessness from inaction**.

It also promotes **emotional regulation**, a cornerstone of psychological well-being.

How It Works

1. Pause to assess the situation.

2. Ask: **What is truly within my control here?**

3. Practice **acceptance** of the rest—without apathy.

4. Take **purposeful action** in your zone of influence.

5. Reflect regularly to strengthen discernment.

Over time, this becomes a habit of thought—**responsive rather than reactive**.

Application

- **Leadership**: Making wise, balanced decisions under pressure.

- **Mental health**: Managing anxiety, depression, or loss.

- **Relationships**: Letting go of control over others' behaviour.

- **Crisis management**: Stabilizing focus and action in uncertainty.

Key Insights

- Not everything deserves your energy.

- Acceptance is not weakness—it's wisdom.

- Knowing the difference is a daily discipline.

- Inner peace often comes from **focused surrender**.

- Discernment is the bridge between **serenity and strength**.

In essence, the **Serenity Prayer Model** teaches us to live wisely by directing effort where it matters—and releasing the rest with grace.

94. Non-Zero-Sum Thinking

Non-Zero-Sum Thinking is a mental model that encourages the recognition of **mutual benefit** in interactions, emphasizing that not all situations require winners and losers. Unlike **zero-sum thinking**—where one person's gain is perceived as another's loss—non-zero-sum thinking sees **collaboration, cooperation, and shared growth** as possible, even preferable. This mindset underlies successful negotiations, partnerships, social progress, and innovation.

Theoretical Basis

The model originates in **game theory**, where outcomes can be classified as:

- **Zero-sum**: One party's gain equals another's loss (e.g., poker).

- **Non-zero-sum**: Gains and losses are not strictly inverse—**both parties can win** (e.g., trade agreements, friendships, or team projects).

Robert Wright's book *Nonzero: The Logic of Human Destiny* explores how human evolution, culture, and technological advancement are driven by the increasing prevalence of non-zero-sum dynamics. Societies evolve by expanding circles of cooperation—families, tribes, nations, and global systems.

Example

Think of two competing tech companies. In a zero-sum mindset, each views the other as a threat—hoarding information, undermining trust, and racing to outdo the other. But in a non-zero-sum approach, they might collaborate on **industry standards or shared platforms**, benefiting both through broader market expansion, improved interoperability, and innovation.

Another example is a marriage: if one partner succeeds in their career, it can benefit both financially and emotionally. Their gain is not a threat to the other—it's a win for the partnership.

Why It Works

Non-zero-sum thinking works because it **amplifies potential gains**, opens paths for **creative problem-solving**, and builds **long-term trust**. It's rooted in the idea that many of life's most valuable outcomes—like love, knowledge, wealth, or innovation—are **expandable, not finite**. Rather than fighting over slices, this model asks, "How can we grow the pie together?"

It also reduces conflict by reframing goals as **interdependent**, not oppositional.

How It Works

The mindset involves:

1. Identifying shared or complementary interests.

2. Reframing problems as **mutual opportunities**.

3. Building systems or agreements where **value is co-created**.

4. Encouraging transparency, trust, and long-term vision.

It shifts behaviour from competition to **strategic collaboration**.

Application

- **Business and negotiation**: Win-win deals, joint ventures, alliances.

- **Diplomacy and politics**: Peace treaties, climate agreements.

- **Personal relationships**: Shared goals and mutual support.

- **Education and teamwork**: Cooperative learning, peer support.

Key Insights

- Not all success is zero-sum—many systems allow **everyone to benefit**.

- Collaboration often creates more value than competition.

- Empathy and trust are crucial to co-creating outcomes.

- Non-zero-sum strategies are foundational to **evolving societies**.

- Thinking beyond scarcity unlocks new opportunities.

In essence, **Non-Zero-Sum Thinking** invites us to move from rivalry to **reciprocity**, turning "either/or" into **"both/and"**.

95. Acceptance and Commitment

Acceptance and Commitment is a psychological framework and mental model rooted in **Acceptance and Commitment Therapy (ACT)**. It encourages individuals to **accept difficult thoughts and emotions**, rather than avoid or suppress them, while **committing to values-driven actions**. The core idea is that **psychological flexibility**—the ability to stay open, present, and aligned with one's values—is the key to long-term well-being and resilience.

Theoretical Basis

Developed by psychologist **Steven C. Hayes**, ACT is grounded in **relational frame theory**, which explores how humans relate to language, thoughts, and experience. Unlike traditional cognitive-behavioural models that seek to change or control negative thoughts, ACT teaches individuals to **observe their thoughts without attachment**, and to act meaningfully despite internal discomfort.

The model revolves around six key processes:

1. **Acceptance** – Opening up to unpleasant experiences.

2. **Cognitive defusion** – Separating from unhelpful thoughts.

3. **Being present** – Mindful awareness of the current moment.

4. **Self-as-context** – Observing oneself from a broader perspective.

5. **Values** – Clarifying what truly matters.

6. **Committed action** – Taking steps aligned with values.

Example

Imagine someone struggling with anxiety about public speaking. Traditional thinking might focus on reducing anxiety before stepping on stage. The ACT approach, however, invites them to **accept the anxiety**, recognize it doesn't have to dictate behaviour, and **commit to giving the speech** because it aligns with a deeper value—like personal growth or helping others.

They're not waiting for anxiety to disappear; they're choosing to act **with** it.

Why It Works

This model works because **resistance to pain often amplifies suffering**. When we try to suppress, fight, or avoid unwanted thoughts or feelings, we often become more entangled in them. Acceptance and Commitment allows people to break that cycle, increasing their ability to **live meaningfully in the presence of discomfort**.

It also shifts the focus from controlling emotions to pursuing what genuinely matters—**building a life around purpose rather than fear**.

How It Works

1. Notice distressing thoughts or feelings.

2. Practice **acceptance** and **defusion**—letting them come and go without control.

3. Return attention to the **present moment**.

4. Identify core **values** that matter.

5. Take **committed action** aligned with those values—even in discomfort.

This cultivates **resilience, authenticity, and momentum**.

Application

- **Therapy and coaching**: Treating anxiety, depression, and burnout.

- **Leadership**: Acting with courage in uncertain or high-stakes situations.

- **Health and fitness**: Committing to habits despite motivational lows.

- **Creativity and innovation**: Pushing forward through fear of failure.

Key Insights

- Discomfort is part of growth, not a signal to stop.

- You don't need to control thoughts to act with purpose.

- Acceptance frees energy for what matters most.

- Clarity of values anchors decision-making.

- Psychological flexibility is a **core skill for modern life**.

In essence, **Acceptance and Commitment** teaches us how to **live fully and meaningfully—even when life is messy**.

96. Resilience Banking

Resilience Banking is a mental model that treats **resilience as a form of stored capital**, much like a bank account. Just as you deposit money into a savings account for future use, you can make **"resilience deposits"**—actions, habits, and mindsets that build up your capacity to withstand stress, adversity, and unexpected setbacks. When challenges arise, you make "withdrawals" from this emotional, mental, and physical reserve.

Theoretical Basis

This model is rooted in principles from **positive psychology**, **stress adaptation theory**, and **systems thinking**. It integrates the idea that resilience is not merely a fixed trait but a **developable resource**. Over time, individuals can build resilience by accumulating protective factors such as strong relationships, coping skills, rest, and meaning-making.

In this context, **resilience = the ability to bounce back + the ability to grow through stress**. The concept encourages intentional preparation for adversity rather than reactive recovery after it hits.

Example

Consider a professional facing a high-pressure project. If they've built up resilience through regular exercise (physical deposit), journaling (emotional deposit), strong social support (relational deposit), and mindfulness practice (mental deposit), they're much more capable of navigating the stress effectively. They're withdrawing from a well-funded "resilience bank." On the other hand, someone with poor sleep, no support system, and unmanaged stress is "overdrawn" and more likely to burn out or break down.

Why It Works

Resilience Banking works because it shifts resilience from an abstract trait to a **tangible investment strategy**. It empowers people to take **proactive control** over their future emotional capacity, much like saving money offers financial security. By consistently making deposits, individuals increase their **adaptive bandwidth**, giving them more tools and stamina when adversity strikes.

It also reinforces the understanding that **resilience isn't built in crisis—it's revealed there**.

How It Works

The model functions by:

1. **Identifying core resilience categories**: emotional, physical, mental, social, and spiritual.

2. **Making small, consistent deposits**: rest, gratitude, connection, reflection, boundaries.

3. **Recognizing withdrawals**: stress, trauma, conflict, overwork.

4. **Maintaining balance**: replenishing deposits regularly, especially after high withdrawal periods.

It encourages **habitual, preventative care**, not just emergency fixes.

Application

- **Leadership**: Building team resilience through shared rituals and psychological safety.

- **Education**: Teaching students self-regulation and coping strategies.

- **Healthcare**: Preventing burnout through self-care planning.

- **Personal growth**: Daily habits that sustain long-term well-being.

Key Insights

- Resilience is a **bankable resource**, not a fixed trait.

- Small, daily actions create large reserves over time.

- Withdrawals are inevitable—deposits must be intentional.

- Balanced systems **bend, not break**, under pressure.

- You must invest in resilience **before you need it most**.

In essence, **Resilience Banking** teaches us that thriving through adversity starts with **consistent, mindful investment in our inner reserves**.

97. Immunity to Change

Immunity to Change is a psychological and developmental model that explains **why people and organizations struggle to implement change**, even when they are genuinely committed to it. Developed by **Robert Kegan** and **Lisa Lahey,** this model suggests that beneath the surface of our conscious goals lie **hidden, competing commitments** and **deep assumptions** that act like an immune system—resisting change to protect our psychological equilibrium.

Theoretical Basis

The model is built on **constructive-developmental theory,** which views human development as an ongoing process of meaning-making. According to Kegan and Lahey, when individuals set goals for improvement but fail to make progress, it's not due to laziness or lack of willpower, but because of a **subconscious system of protection** working to maintain internal consistency and avoid perceived threats.

This internal "immunity" operates just like a biological immune system—blocking foreign elements (in this case, change) to maintain stability.

Example

Imagine a leader who says they want to delegate more to empower their team. However, they continue to micromanage. Their stated goal conflicts with a hidden belief: *"If I don't control everything, I'll be seen as incompetent."* The real barrier to change is not the skill of delegation, but the **fear of vulnerability** tied to an unspoken commitment to appear flawless.

Until that hidden commitment is revealed and re-examined, no amount of surface-level behaviour change will stick.

Why It Works

This model works because it addresses the **root cause of resistance**. Traditional change efforts focus on action plans, goals, and motivation—but Immunity to Change reveals the **emotional and psychological forces** that sabotage progress. By surfacing these inner conflicts, individuals can begin to **dismantle limiting assumptions** and genuinely transform.

It also honours the idea that resistance is **not failure**, but a form of self-protection.

How It Works

The model follows a structured process:

1. **Identify a genuine improvement goal**.

2. **Observe counterproductive behaviours**.

3. **Uncover hidden competing commitments**.

4. **Surface and test big assumptions** underlying those commitments.

Once these assumptions are brought into conscious awareness, they can be challenged and reframed, allowing for meaningful growth.

Application

- **Leadership coaching**: Helping leaders overcome internal blocks.

- **Organizational change**: Addressing cultural resistance to transformation.

- **Education and personal growth**: Shifting long-held beliefs to enable new learning.

- **Therapy**: Rewiring self-limiting mindsets.

Key Insights

- Change resistance is often **protective, not defiant**.

- Competing commitments are usually **unconscious** but powerful.

- Sustainable change requires **deep reflection**, not just surface action.

- Challenging assumptions unlocks real transformation.

- Growth requires both **courage and compassion** for oneself.

In essence, **Immunity to Change** reveals that real change isn't just about doing differently—it's about **thinking and believing differently first**.

98. Psychological Capital

Psychological Capital (PsyCap) is a positive psychology mental model that focuses on the development and application of internal psychological resources that enhance **performance, well-being, and resilience**. Introduced by **Fred Luthans** and colleagues, Psychological Capital goes beyond traditional economic or human capital by emphasizing **who you are and what you can become**, especially in the face of challenge.

Theoretical Basis

Psychological Capital is built on four key components, often referred to by the acronym **HERO**:

1. **Hope** – The ability to set goals, find pathways to reach them, and stay motivated.

2. **Efficacy** – Confidence in your ability to accomplish tasks and overcome challenges.

3. **Resilience** – The capacity to bounce back and grow from adversity.

4. **Optimism** – A realistic, positive outlook on success and the future.

Together, these traits form a **synergistic core** that supports performance, persistence, and emotional health across various life domains.

Example

Imagine two employees facing the same high-pressure project. The one with high PsyCap believes they can succeed (efficacy), sees a clear path forward (hope), remains positive despite setbacks (optimism), and recovers quickly from stress (resilience). The other, with low PsyCap, feels overwhelmed, doubts their abilities, and becomes disengaged. Over time, these differences in mindset lead to vastly different outcomes in performance, motivation, and career growth.

Why It Works

Psychological Capital works because it taps into the **internal psychological resources** that enable people to sustain effort, adapt to pressure, and remain solution-focused. Unlike personality traits, PsyCap components are **state-like**, meaning they are **developable and trainable**. This makes it a powerful tool for personal growth and organizational development.

It enhances well-being, buffers against burnout, and leads to better decision-making under stress.

How It Works

PsyCap is developed and reinforced through:

- **Goal-setting and pathway planning** (for hope).
- **Skill mastery and positive feedback** (for efficacy).

- **Cognitive reframing and support systems** (for resilience).

- **Positive self-talk and learning from success** (for optimism).

Training programs, coaching, and reflective practices can increase PsyCap significantly over time.

Application

- **Leadership development**: Building resilient, hopeful, and confident leaders.

- **Education**: Helping students manage setbacks and persist through learning challenges.

- **Mental health**: Strengthening coping strategies and future orientation.

- **Team performance**: Fostering a collective sense of optimism and resilience.

Key Insights

- Psychological Capital is a **trainable inner resource**, not a fixed trait.

- HERO traits interact and reinforce one another.

- High PsyCap leads to **better outcomes in stress, work, and relationships**.

- Investing in mindset pays off in **resilience, engagement, and innovation**.

- It empowers people to thrive—not just survive—in complex environments.

In essence, **Psychological Capital** is the inner wealth that fuels sustained success, **especially when times get tough**.

99. Grit

Grit is a psychological mental model that refers to the combination of **passion and perseverance** for long-term goals. Popularized by psychologist **Angela Duckworth**, grit is not about quick bursts of effort or talent, but about the **sustained commitment** to work through challenges, setbacks, and monotony in the pursuit of meaningful objectives.

Theoretical Basis

Grit stems from **positive psychology** and challenges the traditional focus on IQ or innate talent as predictors of success. Duckworth's research found that high achievers in areas like education, business, athletics, and the military often shared one trait: a persistent, long-term pursuit of goals despite failure, boredom, or slow progress.

Grit consists of two key components:

1. **Passion** – A deep, enduring interest in a goal or field.

2. **Perseverance** – The ability to stick with effort and overcome obstacles over time.

Example

Consider a young musician aiming to become a concert pianist. Talent may give her a head start, but it's years of daily practice, setbacks, and repetitive drills—without losing enthusiasm—that lead to mastery. When others might quit due to boredom or difficulty, grit keeps her going. Her journey reflects the mental model of grit: **resilient passion plus disciplined effort**.

Duckworth's famous example is the U.S. Military Academy at West Point. Cadets with the highest "grit scores" were more likely to succeed in intense training programs than those with higher SAT scores or athletic ability.

Why It Works

Grit works because **success in complex, long-term pursuits often requires more than intelligence or skill**—it demands **stamina, resilience, and intrinsic motivation**. Gritty individuals don't just show up when things are easy; they persist when progress is slow, results are uncertain, and motivation fades.

It transforms setbacks into fuel, and failure into feedback.

How It Works

Grit operates through:

1. **Goal alignment** – Focusing on deeply held, consistent long-term objectives.

2. **Effort over time** – Treating effort as a multiplier of talent.

3. **Growth mindset** – Belief that abilities can improve with effort.

4. **Emotional regulation** – Staying calm and committed despite obstacles.

It's built like a muscle—through daily choices, habits, and perspective.

Application

- **Education**: Helping students value effort and persistence over grades.

- **Career development**: Sustaining focus over years to build expertise.

- **Athletics**: Training through plateaus and setbacks.

- **Entrepreneurship**: Enduring early-stage failure and uncertainty.

Key Insights

- Grit often outperforms talent in long-term success.

- Passion must be coupled with perseverance to create impact.

- Grit grows through deliberate practice and purpose.

- Failure is part of the process, not the end.

- Long-term achievement requires emotional stamina.

In essence, **Grit** is the quiet force behind greatness—**the decision to keep going when it would be easier to stop**.

100. Emotional Bank Account

The **Emotional Bank Account** is a powerful metaphor for **trust and relationship management**, introduced by **Stephen R. Covey** in his influential book *The 7 Habits of Highly Effective People*. It frames emotional connections as a kind of **bank account**, where every interaction is either a **deposit (positive action)** or a **withdrawal (negative action)** that impacts the overall balance of trust, goodwill, and mutual respect in any relationship.

Theoretical Basis

The model is based on **reciprocity, empathy, and consistency**. Just like a financial bank account, a healthy emotional balance is built gradually through consistent, trustworthy behaviour. Deposits might include acts of kindness, keeping promises, listening attentively, or showing empathy. Withdrawals, on the other hand, occur through broken promises, criticism, neglect, or betrayal.

When the emotional balance is high, the relationship can **withstand conflict, misunderstandings, or stress**. When it's low or overdrawn, even small mistakes can cause major harm, triggering defensiveness, resentment, or disengagement.

Example

Consider a team leader who regularly checks in with team members, celebrates achievements, and shows appreciation. Over time, these positive actions build trust. One day, the leader must deliver tough feedback. Because their emotional bank account is strong, the team receives the criticism constructively.

Contrast this with a manager who rarely acknowledges effort, misses one-on-ones, and gives only negative feedback. Even a minor request or critique may be met with resistance or resentment, because the emotional bank account is already overdrawn.

Why It Works

It works because relationships are **emotionally dynamic**. People need to feel valued, respected, and safe to maintain healthy bonds—whether personal or professional. The Emotional Bank Account model helps people understand the **cumulative impact** of small actions over time and why some relationships thrive while others falter.

It also emphasizes **intentionality**: trust doesn't just happen—it's built through deliberate, empathetic behaviour.

How It Works

The model operates through:

1. **Consistent deposits**: Listening, empathy, honesty, and kindness.

2. **Minimizing withdrawals**: Avoiding blame, broken commitments, or disrespect.

3. **Repairing damage**: Apologizing sincerely and making amends after a withdrawal.

Just like money, emotional capital needs careful management.

Application

- **Leadership**: Building trust with employees and teams.

- **Marriage and parenting**: Strengthening emotional connection and resilience.

- **Customer service**: Cultivating loyalty through care and reliability.

- **Conflict resolution**: Drawing on emotional reserves to heal breaches.

Key Insights

- Trust is built in **small, repeated acts**.

- Withdrawals hurt more when the balance is low.

- High-trust relationships are more **resilient and productive**.

- Apologies and repairs are essential for restoring balance.

- Emotional investment is a **long-term strategy**, not a one-time fix.

In essence, the **Emotional Bank Account** reminds us that relationships thrive on **empathy, consistency, and care**—and every interaction counts.

So the book should really stop here. We've hit 100 Mental Models. That's what you paid for.

But if we stop here then YOU would not experience

Positive Surprise Asymmetry
would YOU ???

Onwards READER !!!! >>>>>

BONUS MENTAL MODELS

Bonus 1. Positive Surprise Asymmetry

Positive Surprise Asymmetry is a mental model rooted in behavioural economics and strategic communication. It refers to the **disproportionately positive emotional and psychological impact** of outcomes that **exceed expectations**. In essence, when people receive **more than they anticipated**, the perceived value and satisfaction are often far greater than if they had simply received what they expected—even if the tangible difference is small.

This model focuses on **under-promising and over-delivering** as a strategy for building trust, delighting others, and influencing perception.

Theoretical Basis

This concept builds on research in **prospect theory** (Daniel Kahneman and Amos Tversky), which shows that people respond to gains and losses **relative to expectations**, not absolute outcomes. If reality exceeds those expectations, the positive emotional response is amplified—often far more than the objective gain would suggest. This "asymmetry" highlights how **managing expectations** is as important as delivering results.

It also ties into **hedonic adaptation**—people quickly normalize predictable outcomes, but surprises spike emotional impact.

Example

Imagine you're told a package will arrive in seven days, but it arrives in three. You're pleasantly surprised, and your satisfaction is high—even if the product itself hasn't changed. Now imagine the reverse: you're promised delivery in two days, but it arrives in three. The result is the same, but disappointment sets in because **expectation management failed**.

Companies like Amazon, Zappos, and Apple often leverage this model—by quoting conservative timelines or outcomes and then beating them, they trigger loyalty and delight.

Why It Works

Positive Surprise Asymmetry works because it taps into the **emotional reward system**. People tend to **anchor** their expectations and assess value based on **relative difference**, not the absolute outcome. When expectations are exceeded, this difference generates **trust, delight, and increased perceived competence**.

It creates memorable moments, which are critical in **building brand loyalty, influence, or relationships**.

How It Works

1. **Set expectations slightly lower than your actual capacity.**

2. **Execute at or above your true ability or promise.**

3. Deliver results that **exceed what was anticipated**, not just what was needed.

4. Use surprise **selectively** so it retains emotional potency.

Application

- **Customer service**: Delivering early, upgrading unexpectedly, or adding value.

- **Leadership**: Promising achievable goals, then surpassing them to boost morale.

- **Relationships**: Thoughtful, unexpected gestures that exceed norms.

- **Negotiation**: Offering more than expected to build goodwill.

Key Insights

- Perception is shaped by **expectation gaps**.

- Surprising upward deviations create **lasting positive impressions**.

- Overpromising sets you up for failure—even with decent results.

- Under-promising strategically allows **room for delight**.

- Used ethically, it builds **trust, loyalty, and influence**.

In essence, **Positive Surprise Asymmetry** is the art of **strategic humility and intentional generosity**, turning modest gains into outsized goodwill.

Bonus 2. Rate of Adaptation

Rate of Adaptation is a mental model that describes how quickly an individual, organization, species, or system can **adjust to changing conditions**—and how that speed of adjustment often determines long-term success or survival. It's not just about recognizing change, but about the **capacity and velocity to respond effectively** to it.

This model underscores that in a rapidly evolving world, **adaptability beats rigidity**, and speed often beats strength.

Theoretical Basis

The concept draws from **evolutionary biology**, particularly the idea that it's not the strongest or smartest species that survives, but the one **most responsive to change**. In business and strategy, it aligns with **agility, feedback loops**, and **learning curves**. In psychology, it reflects **cognitive flexibility** and **resilience**.

The Rate of Adaptation is influenced by:

- **Detection speed** (how fast you notice change),

- **Decision speed** (how fast you interpret and decide),

- **Implementation speed** (how fast you act on it).

Example

Consider Netflix. It started as a DVD rental service, but as technology and consumer habits shifted, it adapted into a streaming platform—and later, into content production. Blockbuster, once the market leader, failed to adapt quickly enough and collapsed. Netflix's **rate of adaptation** was higher, not because it had more resources initially, but because it recognized and moved with changing dynamics faster.

This applies in nature too. The **peppered moth** in England changed coloration as pollution levels altered the environment, giving it a survival advantage over slower-adapting species.

Why It Works

The Rate of Adaptation works because **change is constant**—in markets, environments, technology, and human behaviour. Those who can learn, pivot, or evolve faster maintain relevance and competitive edge. When the environment shifts, even a strong or well-established player can become obsolete if it fails to adjust quickly.

High adaptability enhances resilience, while low adaptability increases fragility.

How It Works

1. **Stay alert** to early signals of change (data, trends, feedback).

2. Maintain **flexible structures** that allow for quick shifts.

3. Encourage a **growth mindset**—treat failure as feedback.

4. Reduce internal friction—eliminate bottlenecks to fast action.

5. **Iterate constantly**—small changes compound adaptability.

Application

- **Startups and business strategy**: Pivoting in response to customer behaviour or market trends.

- **Personal development**: Upskilling and emotional resilience.

- **Technology and design**: Agile development and rapid prototyping.

- **Policy-making and governance**: Responding to crises or societal shifts.

Key Insights

- Speed of adaptation often trumps size or experience.

- Systems that adapt faster gain **compounding advantages**.

- Rigidity in a changing world is a liability.

- Learning loops fuel adaptability—**observe, test, learn, repeat**.

- Adaptation is not a one-time shift, but a **continuous capability**.

In essence, the **Rate of Adaptation** determines whether you're **outpaced or outlasting** in a world that doesn't stand still.

Bonus 3. Coordination Game

The **Coordination Game** is a mental model from **game theory** that explains how individuals or groups achieve optimal outcomes by **aligning their actions** with others. Unlike competitive games where one player's gain is another's loss, coordination games focus on **mutual benefit** through **shared strategies and expectations**. Success depends not just on what you choose, but on how well your choice **matches the choices of others**.

Theoretical Basis

In game theory, a coordination game involves multiple players choosing between options where **payoffs are maximized when choices align**. Each participant has a preference for coordination over conflict. The classic example is the **"driving side" problem**: it doesn't matter whether everyone drives on the left or right side—what matters is that **everyone chooses the same side**.

These games often have multiple equilibria (i.e., more than one "correct" way to coordinate), but the challenge lies in reaching **a shared understanding** of which outcome to pursue.

Example

Consider two friends trying to meet in a city without prior planning. Each must guess where the other is likely to go. If both pick the most prominent landmark (e.g., the train station), they meet successfully. The decision is less about preference and more about **mutual prediction**.

In business, a coordination game can emerge in **technology standards**. Competing companies may prefer different formats, but eventually converge on one (like USB or Blu-ray), because widespread adoption creates network benefits for all users and producers.

Why It Works

The model works because **coordination reduces friction, redundancy, and conflict**. It enables scale, efficiency, and shared value creation. Coordination games also highlight the importance of **social signals, trust, and conventions** in driving collective action. People benefit when they can anticipate and align with the behaviour of others.

In markets, society, and even traffic systems, coordination enables **order without centralized control**.

How It Works

1. **Recognize the interdependence** of choices.

2. **Signal intentions** or interpret signals from others.

3. Align on **focal points**—obvious or established choices.

4. Build **trust and feedback mechanisms** to reinforce alignment.

5. Create **institutions or norms** to support consistent coordination.

The key is achieving **mutual belief** in what the other will do.

Application

- **Standards and protocols**: Tech platforms, safety regulations.

- **Team dynamics**: Aligning roles and workflows.

- **Negotiations**: Settling on fair, mutually beneficial outcomes.

- **Social behaviour**: Norms around etiquette, language, or behaviour.

Key Insights

- Coordination thrives on **shared expectations**.

- Multiple solutions may exist—but agreement is what matters.

- Focal points and social norms guide alignment.

- Trust, clarity, and communication reduce miscoordination.

- Efficient systems often rely on **spontaneous, decentralized coordination**.

In essence, the **Coordination Game** teaches that the best outcomes often come not from competition, but from **synchronization**—acting together toward a shared goal.

Bonus 4. Information Decay

Information Decay is a mental model that refers to the **deterioration of the accuracy, relevance, or value of information over time**. As environments change, data becomes outdated, assumptions become invalid, and insights lose their reliability. This decay can lead to poor decisions if individuals or organizations rely on **stale or contextually obsolete information**.

This model is especially important in the modern era, where rapid technological, economic, and social shifts can render yesterday's truths **misleading or even harmful** today.

Theoretical Basis

Information Decay has roots in **information theory**, **epistemology**, and **systems thinking**. It parallels the concept of **entropy** in physics—over time, systems (and the information they carry) tend to move toward disorder. In organizations, this appears as:

- Memos based on outdated policies

- Strategies based on last year's market data

- Assumptions formed before key environmental changes

Without intentional updating, information becomes **increasingly unreliable**, leading to degraded decisions, inefficient systems, and misaligned actions.

Example

Imagine a company using customer data from five years ago to drive current marketing campaigns. That data may no longer reflect real buying behaviour, preferences, or demographics. Decisions based on it will likely underperform.

Similarly, if a pilot receives old weather information during a flight, it could lead to unsafe navigation decisions. In both cases, the **timeliness and relevance of information are as crucial as its accuracy**.

Why It Works

The model works because it highlights a hidden source of failure: **the silent erosion of information quality**. Many people assume that once something is "known," it remains valid. But in reality, **environments evolve**, making even once-reliable data misleading if it's not regularly refreshed or contextually reviewed.

By recognizing information decay, individuals and systems can **prioritize continuous learning, feedback, and data validation**.

How It Works

1. **Track the age of key data and insights.**

2. Assess whether the **context or environment has shifted**.

3. Revalidate or update data periodically.

4. Favor **live data** and dynamic dashboards over static reports.

5. Build systems that flag or sunset outdated information.

Decision frameworks must integrate **feedback loops and real-time updates** to stay effective.

Application

- **Business strategy**: Refreshing customer, competitor, and market analysis.

- **Healthcare**: Updating medical guidelines based on new research.

- **Technology**: Using current cybersecurity intel, not past threat models.

- **Personal learning**: Revisiting past beliefs or facts as new information emerges.

Key Insights

- Information ages—sometimes faster than we expect.

- Old data can be **more dangerous than no data** if unmarked.

- Fast-changing environments require **frequent reassessment**.

- Systems should be designed for **refresh, not rigidity**.

- Good judgment requires not just data, but **valid, timely data**.

In essence, the **Information Decay** model reminds us that **knowledge has a shelf life**, and staying sharp means staying current.

Bonus 5. Focus Dilution Principle

The **Focus Dilution Principle** is a mental model that describes the decline in effectiveness, clarity, and impact that occurs when **attention, effort, or resources are spread too thinly** across multiple priorities or tasks. The principle warns that **the more directions you try to go at once, the less progress you make in any one direction**. In short, **focus is a finite resource**, and dilution leads to mediocrity, burnout, or stalled momentum.

Theoretical Basis

Rooted in **cognitive psychology**, **attention theory**, and **strategic management**, the Focus Dilution Principle reflects limitations of human attention and organizational capacity. Studies in psychology (e.g., Miller's Law) show that the brain can only process a limited number of things effectively at once. Multitasking decreases performance, increases error rates, and leads to decision fatigue.

In business strategy, this principle aligns with the **Pareto Principle (80/20 rule)** and **opportunity cost**—doing too many things often means neglecting the few that actually drive results.

Example

Imagine a startup trying to launch five different products at once. The team's time, budget, and energy are split across design, marketing, and testing for each product. None receive the focused attention needed to succeed. Launches are delayed, quality suffers, and market traction is weak. Compare this to a competitor that channels everything into one high-impact launch—execution is sharper, learning is faster, and results are measurable.

The same applies personally. An individual trying to learn three new skills simultaneously (coding, writing, and playing guitar) often finds themselves making little progress in any, compared to someone who focuses on one skill at a time with intensity.

Why It Works

The Focus Dilution Principle works because **depth beats breadth** when resources are limited. Concentrated effort creates momentum, mastery, and feedback loops that compound over time. Dilution disperses that energy, leading to inefficiency and diminished results.

By narrowing focus, you enable **higher quality, faster iteration, and deeper insight**—the foundations of excellence.

How It Works

1. **Identify key priorities** that have the highest leverage.

2. Eliminate or defer lower-impact tasks.

3. Channel effort into **one or two key objectives at a time**.

4. Protect attention by minimizing distractions.

5. Reassess regularly and **refocus as needed**.

Application

- **Business strategy**: Prioritizing a core offering before diversifying.

- **Personal productivity**: Using time-blocking and single-tasking.

- **Team leadership**: Aligning team efforts around one clear goal.

- **Learning and growth**: Mastering one skill before moving to the next.

Key Insights

- Focus is a **force multiplier**—it amplifies results.

- Saying "yes" to everything means saying "no" to effectiveness.

- Clarity of purpose enables consistent execution.

- Deep work outperforms scattered effort.

- **Less but better** is the path to mastery and impact.

In essence, the **Focus Dilution Principle** teaches us that **clarity and concentration are the antidotes to overwhelm and underperformance**.

Bonus 6. Network Ignition Point

he **Network Ignition Point** is a mental model that describes the **critical threshold at which a network suddenly becomes self-sustaining, exponential, or valuable**. It reflects the moment when growth shifts from linear to **explosive due to connectivity**, engagement, or scale. Often discussed in the context of technology, social dynamics, and innovation, it applies wherever networks—whether social, informational, biological, or technological—drive value. This model blends insights from **network theory, systems thinking**, and **diffusion of innovation**.

Theoretical Basis

Networks become more valuable as more nodes (people, devices, ideas) are added—a concept captured in **Metcalfe's Law**, which states that a network's value is proportional to the square of its number of users. However, networks don't become powerful immediately. They need to **reach a certain critical mass**—the ignition point—where interactions are rich enough to drive continuous engagement or adoption.

Before the ignition point, progress feels slow and fragile. After it, momentum becomes **self-reinforcing**, often leading to rapid scale.

Example Social media platforms illustrate this well. A new app may struggle for months with limited users. But once it reaches a tipping point—say, when enough users are active daily—network effects take over. More users attract more content, which attracts even more users. This is how platforms like **Facebook**, **TikTok**, or **Clubhouse** grew rapidly after hitting their ignition points.

Similarly, **cryptocurrencies** experience ignition when adoption passes a certain point, enabling liquidity, ecosystem development, and real-world utility.

Why It Works

The model works because networks thrive not on isolated elements but on **connections and interactions**. Early adopters lay the groundwork, but it's the **density of interactions** that triggers ignition. Once the benefits of participation outweigh the cost or friction of joining, others follow—often rapidly.

This shift marks the transition from **push (marketing-driven growth)** to **pull (organic, user-driven growth)**.

How It Works

1. **Seed the network** with early adopters or high-value nodes.

2. Ensure **frictionless interaction** and visible value exchange.

3. Monitor growth and **engagement thresholds**.

4. Once critical mass is reached, amplify via feedback loops.

5. Reinforce stickiness to lock in growth after ignition.

Application

- **Startups and platforms**: Achieving scale via early user networks.

- **Marketing**: Designing referral programs or virality triggers.

- **Product design**: Ensuring usability before scaling.

- **Social movements**: Building support before visible breakthroughs.

Key Insights

- Network value is nonlinear—**nothing happens until it suddenly does**.

- Focus early on **quality of connections**, not just quantity.

- Small, strategic nodes (influencers, niche users) can trigger ignition.

- Ignition requires patience, design, and persistence.

- After ignition, **momentum compounds quickly**—be ready to scale.

In essence, the **Network Ignition Point** teaches that breakthrough often comes not from pushing harder, but from **connecting enough dots until the system catches fire**.

Bonus 7. Adaptive Camouflage

Adaptive Camouflage is a mental model drawn from **biology, evolutionary psychology, and strategy** that describes the ability to **blend into a changing environment by altering appearance, behaviour, or tactics**. It emphasizes **flexibility, observation, and subtlety** as tools for survival, influence, or competitive advantage. In essence, it's about **strategic mimicry and adaptation** to avoid detection, reduce risk, or enhance opportunity in dynamic contexts.

Theoretical Basis

This model originates in **evolutionary biology**, where many organisms survive by changing colour, texture, or behaviour to match their surroundings. From the chameleon to the cuttlefish to the snowshoe hare, adaptive camouflage allows creatures to **avoid predators or sneak up on prey**.

In human systems—such as politics, business, or social dynamics—adaptive camouflage shows up as the ability to **read the room**, adjust tone or strategy, and blend in when necessary to **reduce resistance, observe more clearly, or strategically reposition**.

It is closely related to **situational awareness, strategic silence, and the concept of "masking"** in psychology and sociology.

Example

Consider a new employee entering a high-performing, tight-knit team. Instead of asserting themselves immediately, they spend the first weeks observing, learning the unspoken norms, and adjusting their communication style to match the group's rhythm. Over time, their strategic blending earns trust and positions them to contribute meaningfully without creating friction.

In business, a startup might adopt the visual language or pricing model of an incumbent leader—not to copy blindly, but to reduce adoption resistance and **signal familiarity** to customers.

Why It Works

Adaptive Camouflage works because **fitting in precedes standing out** in many environments. When the cost of being seen as an outsider is high—whether socially, professionally, or competitively—camouflage allows for **strategic patience**, **reduced exposure**, and **greater control** over when and how to reveal differentiation or strength.

It also allows one to **gather intelligence quietly**, without triggering defensive responses.

How It Works

1. **Observe carefully**: Identify environmental cues, social norms, and power dynamics.

2. **Match baseline behaviours or appearances** to avoid premature scrutiny.

3. **Adapt communication style** and presence to fit context.

4. Once embedded, **gradually assert uniqueness or value**.

5. Shift again as the environment evolves.

Application

- **Leadership and diplomacy**: Building rapport before influence.

- **Job interviews or onboarding**: Aligning first, then innovating.

- **Negotiation**: Withholding strength until the right moment.

- **Marketing**: Matching customer language before differentiation.

Key Insights

- **Blend first, stand out later**.

- Early overexposure can trigger resistance or exclusion.

- Camouflage is not deception—it's **strategic alignment**.

- Adaptability is a form of intelligence and control.

- Reading the environment well is **half the battle**.

In essence, **Adaptive Camouflage** teaches that success often starts with **strategic invisibility**, used to quietly gather strength, build trust, and seize the right moment to reveal your full form.

Bonus 8. Optionality

Optionality is a mental model centred around the idea of **maximizing opportunities while minimizing irreversible commitments**. It refers to creating or maintaining **options** that allow you to adapt to uncertainty, pivot when necessary, or capitalize on unexpected upside—all without locking yourself into one rigid path. The goal is to structure life, work, or strategy in ways that **preserve flexibility and increase potential upside**, especially in volatile environments.

Theoretical Basis

Optionality draws from **financial options theory, complexity science**, and **decision theory**. In finance, an option gives you the right—but not the obligation—to buy or sell an asset at a set price in the future. This flexibility has value, particularly in uncertain or high-risk environments.

Philosophers and thinkers like **Nassim Nicholas Taleb** have emphasized optionality as a survival and success mechanism in unpredictable systems. It's deeply linked to **asymmetry**: having more to gain than to lose.

Example

Imagine two professionals. One specializes deeply in a single niche industry; the other builds a broad skill set across several domains—marketing, coding, and design.

When disruption hits the industry, the generalist with more optionality can pivot to a new role, launch a side project, or freelance. The specialist, while once efficient, is now trapped. Optionality gave the generalist more adaptability and resilience.

Startups often apply optionality by testing multiple products or markets before committing fully. Those that succeed preserve their ability to **change direction quickly** if early feedback suggests a better path.

Why It Works

Optionality works because it **reduces downside risk** while preserving or expanding upside potential. In complex, fast-changing environments, it's impossible to perfectly predict the future. By building in options, you position yourself to **benefit from serendipity, randomness, and volatility** rather than being harmed by them.

It's a powerful tool for navigating uncertainty with **agility rather than rigidity**.

How It Works

1. **Create low-cost options**: Side projects, skills, contacts.

2. **Avoid irreversible decisions** unless necessary.

3. **Preserve optionality** by not overcommitting prematurely.

4. **Test ideas early and cheaply** before full investment.

5. **Stay curious** and maintain diverse knowledge and networks.

Application

- **Career planning**: Diversify skills or pursue flexible roles.

- **Investing**: Keep cash or invest in asymmetric bets.

- **Entrepreneurship**: Experiment before scaling.

- **Life design**: Avoid over-optimization for one scenario.

Key Insights

- Flexibility is a form of strength.

- Optionality is most valuable in uncertain, dynamic environments.

- Don't just optimize—**optionize**.

- Saying "yes" too early can destroy future options.

- The best strategies often allow for **future decisions to be made later**.

In essence, **Optionality** teaches us that **freedom of choice and flexibility in action are strategic assets**—especially when the future is unpredictable.

Bonus 9. Signalling Spiral

The **Signalling Spiral** is a mental model that describes how individuals, groups, or organizations engage in **escalating displays of behaviour, belief, or commitment** in order to signal alignment, loyalty, status, or identity. These signals, often public and performative, become increasingly **costly or exaggerated** over time, leading to a spiral effect—where each new signal raises the bar for credibility or inclusion.

Theoretical Basis

This model is rooted in **signalling theory**, a concept from economics and evolutionary biology, which explores how agents send costly signals to convey information that isn't directly observable—like competence, strength, or trustworthiness. The spiral element comes from **feedback dynamics** in social and competitive environments, where individuals feel pressure to **match or exceed others' signals** to maintain status or affiliation.

The Signalling Spiral often results in **over-commitment, performative behaviour**, or **ideological extremity**, not necessarily because participants believe more strongly, but because the environment rewards ever-higher displays.

Example

In social media activism, someone may post a statement supporting a cause. Others follow suit, but soon, statements aren't enough—people begin changing profile pictures, joining protests, or calling out those who are silent. Over time, the cost and intensity of signalling increase. Participants escalate not always out of deeper belief, but to avoid being seen as indifferent or to maintain social standing.

In the corporate world, this can manifest as companies racing to outdo each other with increasingly ambitious sustainability or diversity pledges—not always backed by action, but driven by competitive signalling.

Why It Works

The Signalling Spiral works because **humans are social creatures**, sensitive to reputation, belonging, and perceived authenticity. In many systems, **perception matters as much as reality**. As others raise their signalling, the baseline shifts, creating pressure to keep up or risk being marginalized. The spiral feeds on itself—**each signal sets a new norm**, leading to more dramatic future signals.

It's also reinforced by **status competition**, **peer pressure**, and the desire for moral or ideological clarity.

How It Works

1. Someone sends a signal (belief, behaviour, purchase, post).

2. Others replicate or escalate the signal to match or outdo.

3. The perceived baseline for belonging or credibility rises.

4. Pressure builds to signal even more strongly.

5. Spiral continues until it reaches unsustainable levels or breaks.

Application

- **Politics**: Escalating ideological purity tests.

- **Marketing**: Brands escalating lifestyle claims or ethical positioning.

- **Workplace culture**: Overwork or loyalty signals beyond rational effort.

- **Tribalism**: Group members adopting extreme positions for in-group approval.

Key Insights

- Signals are often more about **identity than information**.

- Escalation can outpace substance or sincerity.

- Watch for **performative pressure** and ask: *Who benefits from the spiral?*

- Spirals can polarize or distort group norms.

- Healthy signalling should remain **anchored to authentic values and proportionality**.

In essence, the **Signalling Spiral** teaches us that when perception becomes currency, **escalation often replaces**

authenticity—and discerning the difference becomes a strategic skill.

Bonus 10. Cognitive Load Saturation

Cognitive Load Saturation mental model:

Cognitive Load Saturation is a mental model that describes the point at which an individual's **mental processing capacity becomes overwhelmed**, leading to **decreased performance, poor decision-making, and higher error rates**. It stems from the understanding that the brain, like any system, has **finite bandwidth** for handling information, attention, and mental effort at any given time.

When cognitive load surpasses this threshold, we enter a state of **saturation**—where adding more tasks, stimuli, or complexity doesn't just reduce efficiency but can actively impair thinking and behaviour.

Theoretical Basis

This model is rooted in **cognitive psychology** and **educational theory**, particularly the work of **John Sweller**, who introduced **Cognitive Load Theory**. The brain has a limited working memory, and when too much information is presented or required simultaneously, it can't process it effectively.

Cognitive load is generally divided into:

1. **Intrinsic load** – the inherent difficulty of the task.

2. **Extraneous load** – distractions or poor information design.

3. **Germane load** – effort related to learning and understanding.

Cognitive Load Saturation occurs when total load exceeds what the mind can handle, resulting in **mental fatigue**, decision paralysis, and even burnout.

Example

Consider an air traffic controller managing multiple aircraft in real time. As more planes enter the airspace, the complexity rises. If the controller's cognitive load exceeds their processing ability—especially under pressure or distraction—the likelihood of error escalates sharply. That's cognitive load saturation.

In everyday life, someone juggling emails, texts, meetings, and project deadlines simultaneously may feel increasingly frazzled. Despite "doing more," they may start missing details or making poor choices.

Why It Works

This model works because it mirrors **real cognitive limitations**. Just as a computer slows down when too many programs are running, the brain becomes less effective when overloaded. Recognizing this limit allows individuals and systems to **prioritize, simplify, and sequence** information more effectively—enhancing clarity and decision quality.

Ignoring saturation leads to **diminishing returns and preventable mistakes.**

How It Works

1. **Assess workload** across tasks and inputs.

2. **Eliminate or defer nonessential tasks** to reduce extraneous load.

3. **Chunk information** into smaller, manageable parts.

4. **Limit context switching** to preserve focus.

5. **Build in recovery** and downtime to reset cognitive capacity.

Application

- **Education**: Designing lessons with clear structure and pacing.

- **Workplace productivity**: Avoiding meeting overload and multitasking.

- **UX/UI design**: Simplifying interfaces to reduce mental effort.

- **Leadership**: Presenting decisions in digestible, non-overwhelming ways.

Key Insights

- The brain has **limited real-time processing power.**

- Multitasking and constant input lead to **mental gridlock**.

- Simplicity and clarity **amplify mental efficiency**.

- Recovery and breaks aren't luxuries—they're **cognitive necessities**.

- Design and communication should respect **mental load limits**.

In essence, **Cognitive Load Saturation** reminds us that **doing more doesn't mean achieving more**—especially when the brain is past capacity.

Bonus 11. Heuristic Overreach

Heuristic Overreach is a mental model that describes what happens when **simple mental shortcuts (heuristics)** are applied **beyond their useful boundaries**, leading to **flawed reasoning or poor decisions**. While heuristics are efficient tools for everyday problem-solving, **overreliance or misuse in complex, unfamiliar, or high-stakes contexts** can lead to cognitive distortions, blind spots, or bias-driven errors.

This model highlights a common trap: **mistaking efficiency for accuracy**, and failing to recognize when a quick mental shortcut is **inadequate or dangerously misleading**.

Theoretical Basis

Heuristics are a key part of **System 1 thinking**, as explained by **Daniel Kahneman and Amos Tversky**. These mental rules-of-thumb evolved to help us make quick judgments under uncertainty. Common heuristics include:

- **Availability heuristic**: Judging likelihood by what's most memorable.

- **Anchoring**: Relying too heavily on the first piece of information.

- **Representativeness**: Judging similarity rather than probability.

Heuristic Overreach occurs when these otherwise useful tools are **used rigidly or without critical evaluation**, especially in domains that require **System 2 thinking** (slow, deliberate reasoning).

Example

Consider a hiring manager who quickly judges candidates based on the "halo effect"—a heuristic where one positive trait (e.g., confident speaking) leads to an assumption of overall competence. In casual settings, this shortcut may save time. But when applied to complex decisions like hiring, it can lead to **overlooking red flags** or choosing someone ill-suited for the role.

In public health, heuristic overreach can show up when people assume a treatment is effective simply because it's "natural," without evaluating scientific evidence—confusing familiarity with efficacy.

Why It Works (and Fails)

Heuristics work well in **stable, familiar, low-risk environments**, where quick judgments usually align with reality. However, when **context shifts**, when stakes are high, or when data is noisy or complex, those same shortcuts become liabilities. Heuristic Overreach fails because it **ignores nuance**, **reduces complexity prematurely**, and **discourages deeper thinking**.

The model matters because many modern challenges—investment decisions, medical diagnoses, strategic planning—require **precision, not just speed**.

How It Works

1. Recognize when a heuristic is being applied.

2. Ask: *Is this situation similar to ones where this heuristic works?*

3. Switch to more analytical methods when novelty, ambiguity, or risk is high.

4. Use heuristics to **triage**, not finalize decisions.

5. Develop **cognitive awareness** to catch misuse.

Application

- **Decision-making**: Slowing down in high-risk or unfamiliar contexts.

- **Leadership**: Avoiding gut-based bias in hiring, policy, or strategy.

- **Education**: Teaching critical thinking to question defaults.

- **Product design**: Not oversimplifying user needs with assumed patterns.

Key Insights

- Heuristics save time—but **cost accuracy if overextended**.

- Familiarity ≠ correctness.

- Awareness of your cognitive tools is as important as their use.

- Good judgment means knowing when **shortcuts aren't enough**.

- Complex problems demand **flexible, not fixed, mental models**.

In essence, **Heuristic Overreach** reminds us that **fast thinking needs boundaries**—and wisdom lies in knowing when to stop and think deeper.

Bonus 12. Cognitive Shortcuts Efficiency

Cognitive Shortcuts Efficiency refers to the human brain's ability to make **quick, efficient decisions using heuristics**— mental shortcuts developed through evolution and experience. These shortcuts allow us to **process complex information rapidly**, often without conscious thought, enabling fast action in situations where speed is more critical than precision.

While often associated with **biases**, cognitive shortcuts are not inherently flawed. In fact, they exist because they **optimize mental energy** and increase decision-making **efficiency** in daily life. This model focuses on how **properly applied heuristics** help navigate information overload, limited time, and uncertain conditions.

Theoretical Basis

Rooted in the work of psychologists **Daniel Kahneman** and **Amos Tversky**, particularly in their studies of **System 1 and System 2 thinking**, this model differentiates between:

- **System 1**: Fast, intuitive, automatic processing (uses shortcuts).

- **System 2**: Slow, deliberate, effortful reasoning.

Cognitive shortcuts (System 1) are essential for handling the thousands of micro-decisions we face each day without overloading our mental capacity.

Example

Imagine you're shopping for a new laptop. You see a familiar brand with great reviews and a mid-range price. Rather than exhaustively comparing every feature of 20 models, you use the **recognition heuristic** (trusted brand), **social proof** (positive reviews), and **price anchoring** to make a decision quickly. You likely won't choose the mathematically optimal product—but you've made a good, efficient choice with minimal effort.

This kind of shortcut is critical in real-life scenarios—like a firefighter instantly recognizing signs of structural collapse or a doctor spotting symptoms that trigger an automatic response.

Why It Works

Cognitive shortcuts work because they **reduce the cognitive load** and speed up decision-making, especially when time or information is limited. They're based on patterns that generally hold true, refined through **experience, repetition, and environmental feedback**.

Rather than aiming for perfection, heuristics aim for **"good enough" solutions with minimal effort**—which in many cases is both practical and sufficient.

How It Works

1. Recognize decision contexts where full analysis is impractical.

2. Use appropriate heuristics (e.g., availability, familiarity, representativeness).

3. Be mindful of **context**—shortcuts work best in familiar, stable environments.

4. Flag high-stakes or novel situations for **System 2 override**.

5. Build "shortcut literacy" to **refine instincts** over time.

Application

- **Productivity**: Rules of thumb for prioritizing tasks.

- **UX/UI design**: Interfaces that align with intuitive mental models.

- **Leadership**: Fast judgments in time-sensitive contexts.

- **Marketing**: Leveraging consumer heuristics like trust signals and framing.

Key Insights

- Heuristics are **not flaws—they're efficiency tools**.

- The brain trades **precision for speed** when appropriate.

- Efficiency comes from recognizing when **"good enough" is truly enough**.

- Over-reliance in unfamiliar contexts leads to bias— **calibrate carefully**.

- Mastery involves **knowing your shortcuts and when to override them**.

In essence, **Cognitive Shortcuts Efficiency** reminds us that **smart simplicity often outperforms over-analysis**, especially in the fast-moving environments we live in.

Bonus 13. Strategic Interdependence

Strategic Interdependence is a mental model that describes situations where the **outcomes of your decisions are directly affected by the decisions of others**, and vice versa. It's a cornerstone concept in **game theory**, **economics**, and **systems thinking**, emphasizing that strategy cannot be developed in isolation—**your best move depends on how others move**.

This model is especially useful in environments where multiple agents—people, teams, companies, or nations— **must anticipate, adapt, and react** to each other's strategies to achieve success.

Theoretical Basis

The roots of this model lie in **game theory**, particularly in the works of **John von Neumann** and **John Nash**. It focuses on **interdependent choices** in games like the Prisoner's Dilemma or competitive business markets. In such systems, each participant must **consider the likely responses of others** when choosing their course of action. The payoff of any decision is not fixed—it **depends on what others choose to do**.

This leads to the need for **anticipation, signalling, collaboration, or competition**, depending on the context.

Example

Imagine two competing airlines considering whether to lower ticket prices. If one lowers prices while the other does not, it may gain market share. But if both lower prices, they risk eroding profits industry-wide. Strategic interdependence forces both to consider not only what's best for themselves but also **what the other party is likely to do in response**. The optimal outcome might be mutual restraint, but without coordination, they may both default to self-defensive price cuts.

This applies broadly—from international relations (arms races) to workplace negotiations or supply chain coordination.

Why It Works

Strategic Interdependence works because it reflects **real-world complexity**, where actions are rarely isolated. It compels decision-makers to **think beyond linear planning** and instead anticipate **second-order effects**, feedback loops, and competitor behaviour.

It prevents naive strategies by highlighting that **success requires adaptation to the dynamics of others**.

How It Works

1. **Map the players**: Identify who else has influence over the outcome.

2. **Understand incentives**: Analyse what each party values or fears.

3. **Anticipate responses**: Forecast how others might react to your moves.

4. **Design interdependent strategies**: Seek alignment, deterrence, or leverage.

5. **Adjust dynamically**: Stay alert to shifts in behaviour or incentives.

Application

- **Business strategy**: Competitive pricing, partnerships, or market entry.

- **Negotiations**: Multi-party talks where perception and trust matter.

- **Public policy**: Climate agreements or trade deals.

- **Organizational leadership**: Cross-team coordination and influence.

Key Insights

- No decision exists in a vacuum—**others' choices shape your results**.

- Mutual success often requires **coordination, not confrontation**.

- Ignoring interdependence leads to **strategic blind spots**.

- Effective strategy requires both **action and anticipation**.

- Systems thrive when **actors align incentives or build trust-based equilibrium**.

In essence, **Strategic Interdependence** reminds us that good strategy is never just about you—it's about how well you **understand and move with others in the system**.

Bonus 14. Marginal Utility Collapse

Marginal Utility Collapse is a mental model that describes the sharp **decline in perceived value or satisfaction** gained from additional units of something—especially when the item or experience is already abundant. It's an extreme version of the **Law of Diminishing Marginal Utility**, where each extra unit yields **less benefit than the one before**, but in this case, the utility doesn't just decrease—it **drops off sharply**, sometimes even becoming negative (e.g., discomfort, waste, regret).

This model is useful for understanding why **more isn't always better**, especially in consumption, wealth, attention, or experience.

Theoretical Basis

Rooted in **economics** and **behavioural psychology**, marginal utility refers to the additional satisfaction derived from consuming one more unit of a good or service. The Law of Diminishing Marginal Utility says that as consumption increases, the added satisfaction from each new unit decreases.

Marginal Utility Collapse goes further. It highlights a **non-linear, often psychological crash** in value—a tipping point where accumulation stops adding benefit and begins to detract from well-being, clarity, or effectiveness.

Example

Imagine eating your favourite dessert. The first few bites are delightful. By the fourth serving, the pleasure has waned. By the sixth, you might feel sick. The **utility collapses**—what once brought joy now brings discomfort.

In digital life, this shows up in **information overload**. Reading one or two insightful articles is helpful. Scrolling through 100 may leave you overwhelmed and anxious— **collapsing the utility** of further input.

Why It Works

Marginal Utility Collapse works because human systems— mental, emotional, physical—have **limits**. Past a certain point, more inputs **overwhelm capacity** or lead to diminishing returns that shift to negative outcomes. This model helps individuals and organizations **optimize for sufficiency**, not just accumulation, and avoid waste or burnout.

It reinforces the principle that **value is contextual** and **non-linear**.

How It Works

1. Recognize areas where more is being pursued without added value.

2. Identify the **saturation point**—when utility sharply drops.

3. Set limits or thresholds to prevent overshoot.

4. Reframe goals around **optimal impact**, not maximal input.

5. Replace accumulation with **curation or refinement**.

Application

- **Time management**: Knowing when more effort produces less (e.g., over-preparing).

- **Design and UX**: Avoiding feature bloat in products.

- **Consumption**: Reducing excess in food, media, or material goods.

- **Productivity**: Prioritizing high-impact actions over sheer volume.

Key Insights

- Value isn't linear—**it often collapses after a point**.

- Awareness of saturation helps prevent regret or inefficiency.

- Simplicity and restraint often produce more sustainable satisfaction.

- Pursuing "more" can cost you what you already have.

- Optimal outcomes come from **knowing when to stop**.

In essence, **Marginal Utility Collapse** reminds us that **wisdom lies in recognizing enough**—and knowing that beyond that, more can become less.

Bonus 15. Perceived Agency Gap

Perceived Agency Gap is a mental model that refers to the **discrepancy between how much control people feel they have over a situation** versus how much control they actually possess. When people perceive themselves as **powerless**, even if they are not, it can lead to inaction, disengagement, or helplessness. Conversely, overestimating agency can result in frustration or misplaced blame when things go wrong.

The core insight is that **our decisions and behaviour are often driven not by real control, but by our *perception* of control**—and that perception can be skewed by design, environment, culture, or past experiences.

Theoretical Basis

This model draws from **psychology**, particularly concepts like **learned helplessness** (Martin Seligman), **locus of control** (Julian Rotter), and **self-efficacy** (Albert Bandura). These theories show that humans tend to act—or not—based on whether they believe their actions influence outcomes. When there is a mismatch between actual and perceived control, decision quality and engagement drop.

Perceived Agency Gap can be artificially widened by systems, institutions, or technologies that obscure consequences, fragment accountability, or reduce feedback.

Example

In a large organization, an employee might stop offering ideas because they believe leadership won't listen—even though management is actively seeking input. This perceived agency gap leads to silence, underperformance, and dissatisfaction, despite the fact that the employee *could* have made a difference. The issue isn't capacity—it's perception.

Similarly, in digital platforms, users might feel voiceless in shaping algorithms or content policies, even when feedback mechanisms exist. If users don't *believe* their voice matters, they won't act.

Why It Works

This model is useful because it explains a hidden driver of behaviour: **people act in line with what they believe they can influence**. When the agency gap is wide, apathy and resentment grow. Narrowing that gap—by clarifying impact or removing barriers—leads to empowerment, motivation, and initiative.

It's especially important in leadership, design, education, and social movements.

How It Works

1. Identify situations where people are disengaged or passive.

2. Assess if there's a mismatch between perceived and actual control.

3. Communicate clearly where and how agency exists.

4. Offer meaningful feedback and visibility of impact.

5. Remove psychological or systemic blockers to action.

Application

- **Leadership**: Empowering teams with clear ownership and feedback loops.

- **UX/UI design**: Making user actions feel impactful and visible.

- **Education**: Reinforcing students' belief in their ability to learn and influence outcomes.

- **Civic engagement**: Closing the gap between voting and policy impact.

Key Insights

- People act based on **perceived**, not actual, control.

- Gaps in agency perception lead to **learned helplessness or disengagement**.

- Empowerment isn't just structural—it's **psychological**.

- Systems that close the agency gap foster **initiative, trust, and innovation**.

- Always ask: *Do people feel like their actions matter here?*

In essence, the **Perceived Agency Gap** teaches us that meaningful engagement starts with helping people **see and believe in their power to act**.

If you enjoyed this 2nd book on 100 mental models then you can catch up with my 1st book on 100 mental models and check back for my forthcoming 3rd book.

Perhaps the 3rd book is already out – check here.

Scan this QR code or follow this short link to get my latest book, or pre-order it.

tinyurl.com/100MentalModels

Hope you got something from this book! Dan

OTHER BOOKS IN THIS 100 SERIES – SCAN HERE

100 COGNITIVE AND MENTAL MODELS TO HELP YOUR CAREER: Mental Shortcuts for Smarter Choices, Sharper Thinking, and Success

-

ANOTHER 100 MENTAL MODELS TO HELP YOUR CAREER - VOLUME 2: Another 100 Powerful Mental Models for Clarity, Confidence, and Climbing the Career Ladder

-

100 HEURISTICS AND HEURISTIC MODELS: The Hidden Rules of Smart Thinking Used by Experts, Entrepreneurs, and Machines

-

100 GAME THEORIES AND DECISION MODELS FOR RATIONAL DECISION MAKING IN COMPETITIVE SITUATIONS: 100 Winning Strategies for Rational Thinking in High-Stakes Scenarios

-

100 BUSINESS STRATEGIES PROVEN TACTICS FOR GROWTH, INNOVATION AND MARKET DOMINATION: Actionable Strategies to Scale, Disrupt and Lead in Any Industry

-

100 LEADERSHIP MODELS AND STRATEGIES FOR EFFECTIVE DECISION-MAKING FOR ORGANIZATIONAL SUCCESS: Empowering Your Leadership, 100 Proven Strategies and Models to Enhance Decision-Making & Drive Success

-

100 BUSINESS GROWTH HACKS AND STRATEGIES TO GROW PROFIT AND INCREASE YOUR COMPETITIVE ADVANTAGE: Proven Techniques to Scale Faster, Boost Revenue, and Dominate Your Market with Actionable Growth

-

100 ECONOMIC THEORIES DEMYSTIFIED : A Guide To The World's Most Influential Economic Ideas From Keynesian Economics To Debt-deflation Theory

-

100 PASSIVE INCOME STREAM SIDE HUSTLES, MASTERING SIDE HUSTLES AND SMART INVESTMENTS: How to Make Money While You Sleep and Secure Your Financial Future

-

WHILST YOU ARE HERE , WHY NOT SCAN THIS TO SEE IF THERE ARE ANY MORE BOOKS PUBLISHED YET

OR FOLLOW ME AT @DANDANMUSICMAN ON X AND @DANDANMUSICMANUK ON INSTAGRAM

100 HEURISTICS + HEURISTIC MODELS

THE HIDDEN RULES OF SMART THINKING USED BY EXPERTS, ENTREPRENEURS, AND MACHINES

100 HEURISTIC MODELS
BY DAN WAITE

BRANCH AND BOUND	VORONOI	MANHATTAN DISTANCE
A* SEARCH	MINIMAX	METAHEURISTICS
SERIAL POSITION	CONTEXT-DEPENDENT	MNEMONIC
RETRIEVAL FLUENCY	SPACED REPETITION	CHUNKING
ADVERSE SELECTION	RULE CHAINING HEURISTIC	MEANS-ENDS ANALYSIS
NORM-FOLLOWING	IN-GROUP BIAS	LEFT-HAND RULE
LEFT-HAND RULE	NAVIGATION AND SPATIAL	EUCLIDEAN DISTANCE
SALIENCE	BASE RATE NEGLECT	AND MANY, MANY MORE

MASTERING SIDE HUSTLES AND SMART INVESTMENTS
SIDE HUSTLES
BY DAN WAITE

SLEEP & MEDITATION SOUNDTRACKS	RENTING OUT DRONES	LONG-TERM BONDS
SOLAR FARM INVESTMENTS	AIRBNB RENTAL ARBITRAGE	SUBSCRIPTION BASED FINANCIAL SERVICES
INVESTING IN TIMBERLAND	AUTOMATED E-COMMERCE	HEDGE FUNDS
PUBLISHING AUDIOBOOKS	AI-POWERED SEO WEBSITES	AUTOMATED PLATFORMS MONEY LENDING
AMAZON FBA BUSINESS	YOUTUBE AUTOMATION CHANNELS	FRANCHISING
TAX LIEN INVESTING	SILENT PARTNERSHIPS	CASHBACK APPS

100 PASSIVE INCOME STREAM GENERATING IDEAS

ELECTRIC BIKE RENTAL STATIONS	AIRPORT PARKING SPACE RENTAL	AUTOMATED BIKE SCOOTER RENTALS
DRONE RENTALS	SEMI-TRUCK LEASING	SOLAR PANEL LEASING
ICE VENDING MACHINES	ARCADE MACHINES	BILLBOARD SPACE
LAUNDROMATS	STORAGE FACILITY OWNERSHIP	ATM MACHINES
SAAS BUSINESS	STOCK MUSIC SALES	PRINT ON DEMAND
WEBSITE FLIPPING	YOUTUBE ADS	COACHING PROGRAMS
AI-GENERATED CONTENT	STOCK VIDEO FOOTAGE SALES	SELF-PUBLISHING BOOKS
VENDING MACHINES	OLD COURSE ROYALTIES	AND MANY, MANY MORE

PROVEN TACTICS FOR GROWTH, INNOVATION, AND MARKET DOMINATION
100 BUSINESS STRATEGIES
BY DAN WAITE

REFERRAL PROGRAM STRATEGY	CUSTOMER-CENTRIC STRATEGY	BOOTSTRAPPING STRATEGY
VENTURE CAPITAL STRATEGY	CROWDFUNDING STRATEGY	PRIVATE EQUITY STRATEGY
DEFENSIVE STRATEGY	HYPERLOCAL STRATEGY	DROPSHIPPING STRATEGY
AUTOMATION STRATEGY	SURPRISE & DELIGHT STRATEGY	HYPERAUTOMATION STRATEGY
REVERSE LOGISTICS STRATEGY	SIX SIGMA STRATEGY	GAMIFICATION STRATEGY
HYPER-PERSONALIZATION STRATEGY	ECOSYSTEM STRATEGY	JUST-IN-TIME (JIT) STRATEGY

100 BUSINESS STRATEGIES

BLUE OCEAN EXPANSION	BLOCKCHAIN STRATEGY	UPSELLING STRATEGY
WEB3 STRATEGY	METAVERSE STRATEGY	SEO STRATEGY
BLUE OCEAN STRATEGY	GLOBAL EXPANSION STRATEGY	CONGLOMERATE STRATEGY
HORIZONTAL INTEGRATION	VERTICAL INTEGRATION	FIRST-MOVER ADVANTAGE
FAST-FOLLOWER STRATEGY	PLATFORM STRATEGY	COST LEADERSHIP STRATEGY
DIFFERENTIATION STRATEGY	ORGANIC GROWTH STRATEGY	GROWTH HACKING STRATEGY
OMNICHANNEL STRATEGY	LOYALTY PROGRAM STRATEGY	VIRAL MARKETING STRATEGY
STORYTELLING STRATEGY	NOSTALGIA MARKETING STRATEGY	AND MANY, MANY MORE

100 GAME THEORIES AND DECISION MODELS
GAME THEORY
BY DAN WAITE

MUTUALLY ASSURED DESTRUCTION	DOLLAR AUCTION	HAWK-DOVE GAME
VOLUNTEER'S DILEMMA	SILENT DUEL	AI ALIGNMENT GAME
BAYESIAN GAME	TIPPING POINT GAME	SOCIAL INFLUENCE
TIT-FOR-TAT IN EVOLUTION	DIVIDE THE DOLLAR GAME	MONTY HALL PROBLEM
DIFFUSION OF RESPONSIBILITY	FREE RIDER PROBLEM	FLOCKING BEHAVIOUR
PARASITE-HOST GAME	CYBERSECURITY GAME	PREDATOR-PREY GAME

100 GAME THEORIES
RATIONAL DECISION-MAKING IN COMPETITIVE SITUATIONS

EVOLUTIONARILY STABLE STRATEGY	LIMITED WAR GAME	SECURITY DILEMMA
TRUST GAME	SUNK COST GAME	SHAPLEY VALUE
TERRORIST VS. GOVERNMENT	SPY VS. SPY GAME	DETERRENCE THEORY GAME
COLONEL BLOTTO GAME	WAR OF ATTRITION	MARKET FOR LEMONS
MORAL HAZARD GAME	PRINCIPAL-AGENT PROBLEM	JOB MARKET SIGNALLING
SOCIAL MEDIA VIRALITY GAME	SPAM DETECTION GAME	ADVERSE SELECTION GAME
BERTRAND COMPETITION	CASCADING FAILURE GAME	EL FAROL BAR PROBLEM
SELF-DRIVING CAR DILEMMA GAMES	MECHANISM DESIGN THEORY	AND MANY, MANY MORE

ORGANIZATIONAL SUCCESS AND EFFECTIVE DECISION-MAKING
100 LEADERSHIP MODELS AND STRATEGIES
BY DAN WAITE

GAMIFICATION LEADERSHIP	NONPROFIT LEADERSHIP	IMPROV LEADERSHIP
HACKER LEADERSHIP	SWARM LEADERSHIP	TECH LEADERSHIP
GREAT MAN THEORY	SITUATIONAL LEADERSHIP	AGILE LEADERSHIP
HOLOGRAPHIC LEADERSHIP	TRANSFORMATIONAL LEADERSHIP	PEER LEADERSHIP
LAISSEZ-FAIRE LEADERSHIP	AUTOCRATIC LEADERSHIP	BENEVOLENT DICTATORSHIP
POLITICAL LEADERSHIP	MILITARY LEADERSHIP	LEVEL FIVE LEADERSHIP

100 LEADERSHIP MODELS

RESONANT LEADERSHIP	COACHING LEADERSHIP	EMPATHETIC LEADERSHIP
AI-INTEGRATED LEADERSHIP	MAVERICK LEADERSHIP	IMPROV LEADERSHIP
VISIONARY LEADERSHIP	PACESETTING LEADERSHIP	SUSTAINABLE LEADERSHIP
PARADOXICAL LEADERSHIP	INFLUENCER LEADERSHIP	OPEN-SOURCE LEADERSHIP
STOIC LEADERSHIP	ZEN LEADERSHIP	STARTUP LEADERSHIP
EXISTENTIAL LEADERSHIP	DIALECTICAL LEADERSHIP	SPIRITUAL LEADERSHIP
HUMAN-CENTERED LEADERSHIP	CRISIS LEADERSHIP	HOLACRACY LEADERSHIP
SPORTS LEADERSHIP	DATA-DRIVEN LEADERSHIP	AND MANY, MANY MORE

100 ECONOMIC THEORIES DEMYSTIFIED
ECONOMIC THEORIES
BY DAN WAITE

MERCANTILISM	GIG ECONOMY THEORY	SAY'S LAW
MALTHUSIAN THEORY	JAPAN'S ECONOMIC MODEL	MARXIST ECONOMICS
RICARDIAN EQUIVALENCE	UTILITY THEORY	MARGINAL UTILITY THEORY
D.O.G.E. DEPARTMENT OF GOVERNMENT EFFICIENCY	GENERAL EQUILIBRIUM THEORY	RANDOM WALK THEORY
PRICE ELASTICITY OF DEMAND	CONSUMER SURPLUS	CLASSICAL ECONOMICS
THEORY OF THE FIRM	PIGOUVIAN TAXES	KEYNESIAN ECONOMICS

100 ECONOMIC THEORIES DEMYSTIFIED

EVOLUTIONARILY STABLE STRATEGY	LIMITED WAR GAME	IRRATIONAL EXUBERANCE
PHILLIPS CURVE	DEBT-DEFLATION THEORY	SHAPLEY VALUE
PERMANENT INCOME HYPOTHESIS	VEBLEN GOODS	BRETTON WOODS SYSTEM
MORAL HAZARD	MARKET STRUCTURE THEORY	DUTCH DISEASE
ADVERSE SELECTION	NETWORK EFFECTS	HARROD-DOMAR GROWTH MODEL
GLOBALIZATION THEORY	GRAVITY MODEL OF TRADE	NEW TRADE THEORY
CONVERGENCE THEORY	HECKSCHER-OHLIN MODEL	SOLOW-SWAN GROWTH MODEL
CREATIVE DESTRUCTION	BIG PUSH THEORY	AND MANY, MANY MORE

HACKS AND STRATEGIES TO GROW PROFIT
100 BUSINESS GROWTH HACKS
BY DAN WAITE

ABANDONED CART HACK	SKYSCRAPER CONTENT HACK	DRIP CAMPAIGN HACK
POLL AND QUIZ HACK	GIVEAWAY COLLAB HACK	F.O.M.O. HACK
SOCIAL PROOF HACK	BRANDED HASHTAG HACK	MICRO-EXPERIMENT HACK
"FIRST NAME PLUS EMOJI HACK"	TREND JACKING HACK	SOCIAL LOCK HACK
SCRAPING AND OUTREACH HACK	STICKER BOMB HACK	STEAL COMPETITOR TRAFFIC HACK
TRIP-WIRE OFFER HACK	MICRO COMMITMENT HACK	GAMIFICATION IN-APP HACK

100 BUSINESS GROWTH HACKS

LOSS AVERSION HACKS	PEOPLE ALSO ASK HACK	ANSWER BOX HACK
LIVE CHAT HACK	INFOGRAPHIC HACK	AI CHATBOT HACK
WIN-BACK CAMPAIGN HACK	FAKE WAITING LIST HACK	YOUTUBE SEO HACK
LEAD MAGNET HACK	PEOPLE ALSO ASK HACK	DRIP CAMPAIGN HACK
AI CONTENT CREATION HACK	REACTIVATION HACK	REDDIT AND QUORA HACK
CROSS PROMOTION HACK	REFERRAL LOOP HACK	TREND JACKING HACK
MEMES AND GIFS HACK	REVERSE FUNNEL HACK	EXIT-INTENT POPUPS HACK
"DARK MODE" HACK	LEADERBOARD HACK	AND MANY, MANY MORE

www.ingramcontent.com/pod-product-compliance
Lightning Source LLC
Chambersburg PA
CBHW060114200326
41518CB00008B/825